Charles Forbes Montalembert

Saint Columba Apostle Of Caledonia

Charles Forbes Montalembert

Saint Columba Apostle Of Caledonia

ISBN/EAN: 9783337330590

Printed in Europe, USA, Canada, Australia, Japan

Cover: Foto ©Lupo / pixelio.de

More available books at **www.hansebooks.com**

"In gentes ego mitto te, aperire oculos eorum, ut convertantur a tenebris ad lucem, et de potestate Satanæ ad Deum, ut accipiant remissionem peccatorum, et sortem inter sanctos."—ACT. xxvi.

SAINT COLUMBA

APOSTLE OF CALEDONIA

BY THE

COUNT DE MONTALEMBERT

OF THE FRENCH ACADEMY

FIDE AC VERITATE

NEW YORK
THE CATHOLIC PUBLICATION HOUSE
126 NASSAU STREET
MDCCCLXVIII

PREFACE.

THE Narrative now given to the public is taken from the Third Volume of the 'Monks of the West,' the first of the three volumes of that work which are dedicated to the conversion of the British Isles by the Celtic and Roman Missionaries. It has appeared to some that the life of St. Columba—one of the most heroic and the least remembered of the combatants in that great conflict—might, without inconvenience, be detached from the rest of the work, and would not on that account be found less wanting in serious and original interest. In accordance with their desire, the following pages are published. It is of importance to bear in mind that everything in this narrative is borne out by the best known records of Irish hagiography. The Author has not written one word which cannot be justified or explained by documents the value of which is proved or discussed in the notes to his larger work. These notes it has been necessary for the most part to exclude from the present reprint, to avoid unnecessarily extending its bulk. But any curious or sceptical reader will do well to consult them in the text of 'The Monks of the West,' before forming his judgment of the men and transactions of the sixth century in Ireland and Scotland.

CONTENTS.

CHAPTER I.

THE YOUTH OF COLUMBA, AND HIS MONASTIC LIFE IN IRELAND.

The biographers of Columba.—His different names.—His royal origin.—The supreme kings of Ireland: the O'Neills and O'Donnells; Red Hugh.—Birth of Columba; vision of his mother.—His monastic education; jealousy of his comrades; Kieran; the two Finnians; the school of Clonard.—Vision of the guardian angel and the three brides.—The assassin of a virgin struck by death at the prayer of Columba.—His youthful influence in Ireland; his monastic foundations, especially at Durrow and at Derry; his song in honour of Derry.—His love for poetry; his connection with the travelling bards.—He was himself a poet, a great traveller, and of a quarrelsome disposition.—His passion for manuscripts.—Longarad of the hairy legs and his bag of books.—Dispute about the Psalter of Finnian; judgment of King Diarmid, founder of Clonmacnoise.—Protest of Columba; he takes to flight, chanting the *Hymn of Confidence*, and raises a civil war.—Battle of Cul-

Dreimhne; the *Cathac* or Psalter of battle.—Synod of Teltown; Columba is excommunicated.—St Brendan takes part with Columba, who consults several hermits, and among others Abban, in the Cell of Tears.—The last of his advisers, Molaise, condemns him to exile.—Twelve of his disciples follow him; devotion of the young Mochonna.—Contradictory reports concerning the first forty years of his life,   .   1

CHAPTER II.

COLUMBA AN EMIGRANT IN CALEDONIA—THE HOLY ISLE OF IONA.

Aspect of the Hebridean archipelago.—Columba first lands at Oronsay, but leaves it because Ireland is visible from its shores.—Description of Iona.—First buildings of the new monastery.—What remains of it.—Enthusiasm of Johnson on landing there in the eighteenth century.—Columba bitterly regrets his country.—Passionate elegies on the pains of exile.—Note upon the poem of *Altus*.—Proofs in his biography of the continuance of that patriotic regret.—The stork comes from Ireland to Iona,   .   .   31

CHAPTER III.

THE APOSTOLATE OF COLUMBA AMONG THE SCOTS AND PICTS.

Moral transformation of Columba.—His progress in spiritual life.—His humility.—His charity.—His preaching by tears.—The hut which formed his abbatial palace at Iona.—His prayers; his work of transcription.—His crowd of visitors.—His severity in the examination of monastic vocations.—Aïdus the Black, the murderer of Columba's enemy King Diarmid, rejected by the community.—Penance of Libran of the Rushes.—Columba encourages the despairing and unmasks the hypocrites.—Monastic propaganda of Iona ; Columba's fifty-three foundations in Scotland.—His relations with the people of Caledonia : First with the colony of Dalriadians from Ireland, whose king was his relative ; he enlightens and confirms their imperfect Christianity.—Ambushes laid for his chastity.—His connection with the Picts, who occupied the north of Britain.—The *dorsum Britanniæ*.—Columba their first missionary.—The fortress gates of their king Brudus open before him.—He struggles with the Druids in their last refuge.—He preaches by an interpreter.—His respect for natural virtue.—Baptism of two old Pictish chiefs.—Columba's humanity : he redeems an Irish captive. — Frequent journeys among the Picts, whose conversion he accomplishes before he dies.—His fellow-workers, Malruve and Drostan ; the Monastery of Tears, ... 43

CHAPTER IV.

COLUMBA CONSECRATES THE KING OF THE SCOTS.—HE GOES TO THE NATIONAL ASSEMBLY OF IRELAND, DEFENDS THE INDEPENDENCE OF THE HIBERNIO-SCOTIC COLONY, AND SAVES THE CORPORATION OF BARDS.

Passionate solicitude of Columba for his relatives and countrymen.—He protects King Aïdan in his struggle with the Anglo-Saxons of Northumbria.—The same king is crowned by Columba at Iona ; the first example of a Christian consecration of kings.—The Stone of Destiny: The descendants of Aïdan.—

Synod or Parliament of Drumceitt in Ireland.—Aedh, king of Ireland, and Aïdan, king of the Irish colonists in Scotland.—The independence of the new Scottish kingdom is recognised through the influence of Columba.—He interposes in favour of the bards, whom the king had proposed to outlaw.—Power and excesses of that corporation.—By means of Columba, the good grain is not burned with the weeds.—The bards' song of gratitude in honour of their saviour.—Columba, reproved by his disciple, desires that this song should not be repeated during his life.—Superstitious regard attached to it after his death.—Intimate union between music, poetry, and religion in Ireland.—The bards, transformed into minstrels, are the first champions of national independence and Catholic faith against the English conquest.—Fiercely assailed, they yet continue to exist up to our own day.—Moore's *Irish Melodies*.—The Celtic muse at the service of the vanquished in the Highlands of Scotland as in Ireland, . . 68

CHAPTER V.

COLUMBA'S RELATIONS WITH IRELAND—CONTINUED.

Cordial intercourse of Columba with the Irish princes.—Prophecy upon the future of their sons.—Domnall, the king's son, obtains the privilege of dying in his bed.—Columba visits the Irish monasteries.—Popular enthusiasm.—Vocation of the young idiot afterwards known as St Ernan.—Solicitude of Columba for the distant monasteries and monks.—He protects them from excessive labours and accidents.—He exercises authority over laymen.—Baithen, his cousin-german and principal assistant.—The respect shown to both in an assembly of learned men, . 87

CHAPTER VI.

COLUMBA, THE PROTECTOR OF SAILORS AND AGRI-
CULTURISTS, THE FRIEND OF LAYMEN, AND THE
AVENGER OF THE OPPRESSED.

His universal solicitude and charity during all his missionary life. — The sailor-monks: seventy monks of Iona form the crew of the monastic fleet; their boats made of osiers covered with hides.—Their boldness at sea: the whirlpool of Corryvreckan.—Columba's prayer protects them against sea-monsters.—Their love of solitude leads them into unknown seas, where they discover St Kilda, Iceland, and the Farœ Isles.—Cormac in Orkney, and in the icy ocean.—Columba often accompanies them: his voyages among the Hebrides.—The wild boar of Skye.—He subdues tempests by his prayer: he invokes his friend St Kenneth. — He is himself invoked during life, and after his death, as the arbiter of winds.—Filial complaints of the monks when their prayers are not granted.—The benefits which he conferred on the agricultural population disentangled from the maze of fables: Columba discovers fountains, regulates irrigations and fisheries, shows how to graft fruit-trees, obtains early harvests, interferes to stop epidemics, cures diseases, and procures tools for the peasants.—His special solicitude for the monkish labourers: he blesses the milk when it is brought from the cow: his breath refreshes them on their return from harvest.—The blacksmith carried to heaven by his alms.—His relations with the layman whose hospitality he claims: prophecy touching the rich miser who shuts his door upon him.—The five cows of his Lochaber host.—The poacher's spear.—He pacifies and consoles all whom he meets.—His prophetic threats against the felons and rievers.—Punishment inflicted upon the assassin of an exile.—Brigands of royal blood put down by Columba at the risk of his life.—He enters into the sea up to his knees to arrest the pirate who had pillaged his friend. — The standard-bearer of Cæsar and the old missionary, . . . 96

CHAPTER VII.

COLUMBA'S LAST YEARS—HIS DEATH—HIS CHARACTER.

Columba the confidant of the joys and consoler of the sorrows of domestic life.—He blesses little Hector with the fair locks.—He prays for a woman in her delivery; he reconciles the wife of a pilot to her husband.—Vision of the saved wife who receives her husband in heaven.—He continues his missions to the end of his life.—Visions before death.—The Angels' Hill.—Increase of austerities.—Nettle-soup his sole food.—A supernatural light surrounds him during his nightly work and prayers.—His death is retarded for four years by the prayers of the community.—When this respite has expired, he takes leave of the monks at their work; he visits and blesses the granaries of the monastery.—He announces his death to his attendant Diarmid.—His farewell to his old white horse.—Last benediction to the isle of Iona; last work of transcription; last message to his community.—He dies in the church. —Review of his life and character, . . . 122

CHAPTER VIII.

SPIRITUAL DESCENDANTS OF ST COLUMBA.

His posthumous glory: miraculous visions on the night of his death: rapid extension of his worship.—His solitary funeral and tomb at Iona.—His translation to Ireland, where he rests between St Patrick and St Bridget.—He is, like Bridget, feared by the Anglo-Norman conquerors.—John de Courcy and Richard Strongbow.—The *Vengeance of Columba.*—Supremacy of Iona over the Celtic churches of Caledonia and the north of Ireland.—Singular privilege and primacy of the abbot of Iona in respect to bishops.—The ecclesiastical organisation of Celtic countries exclusively monastic.—Moderation and respect of Columba for the episcopal rank.—He left behind him no special rule.—That which he followed differed in no respect from the usual customs of the monastic order, which proves the exact observance of all the precepts of the Church, and the chimerical nature of all speculations upon the primitive Protestantism of the Celtic Church.—But he founded an order, which lasted several centuries under the title of the Family of Columb-kill.—The clan and family spirit was the governing principle of Scottish monasticism.—Baithen and the eleven first successors of Columba at Iona were all members of the same race.—The two lines, lay and ecclesiastical, of the great founders.—The headquarters of the order transferred from Iona to Kells, one of Columba's foundations in Ireland.—The *Coarbs.*—Posthumous influence of Columba upon the Church of Ireland.—*Lex Columcille.*—Monastic Ireland in the seventh century the principal centre of Christian knowledge and piety.—Each monastery a school.—The transcription of manuscripts, which had been one of Columba's favourite occupations, continued and extended by his family even upon the continent.—Historic annals.—The *Festiloge* of Angus the Culdee.—The Culdees.—Propagation of Irish monasticism abroad.—Irish saints and monasteries in France, Germany, and Italy.—The Irish saint Cathal venerated in Calabria under the name of *San Cataldo.*—Monastic university of Lismore: crowd of foreign students, especially of Anglo-Saxons, in

Irish monasteries.—Confusion of temporal affairs in Ireland.—Civil wars and massacres.—Notes upon king-monks.—Patriotic intervention of the monks.—Adamnan, biographer and ninth successor of Columba, and his *Law of the Innocents.*—They are driven from their cloisters by the English.—Influence of Columba in Scotland.—Traces of the ancient Caledonian Church in the Hebrides.—Apostolical mission of Kentigern in the country between the Clyde and the Mersey.—His meeting with Columba.—His connection with the king and queen of Strathclyde.—Legend of the queen's ring.—Neither Columba nor Kentigern acted upon the Anglo-Saxons, who continued pagans, and maintained a threatening attitude.—The last bishops of conquered Britain desert their churches, ... 138

ST COLUMBA.

CHAPTER I.

The Youth of Columba and his Monastic Life in Ireland.

T COLUMBA, the apostle and monastic hero of Caledonia, has had the good fortune to have his history written by another monk, almost a contemporary of his own, whose biography of him is as delightful as it is edifying. This biographer, Adamnan, was the ninth successor of Columba as abbot of his principal establishment at Iona, and in addition was related to him. Born only a quarter of a century later, he had seen in his childhood the actual companions of Columba and those who had received his last breath. He wrote at the very fountainhead, on the spot where his glorious prede-

cessor had dictated his last words, surrounded by scenes and recollections which still bore the trace of his presence, or were connected with the incidents of his life. A still earlier narrative written by another abbot of Iona, and reproduced almost word for word by Adamnan, forms the basis of his work, which he has completed by a multitude of anecdotes and testimonies collected with scrupulous care, and which altogether, though unfortunately without chronological order, forms one of the most living, attractive, and authentic relics of Christian history.*

Like twenty other saints of the Irish calendar, Columba bore a symbolical name borrowed from the Latin, a name which signified the dove of the Holy Ghost, and which was soon to be rendered illustrious by his countryman Columbanus, the celebrated founder of Luxeuil, with whom many modern historians have confounded him. To distinguish the one from the other, and to indicate specially the greatest Celtic missionary of the British Isles, we shall adopt, from the different versions of his name, that of Columba. His countrymen have almost always named him *Columb-kill* or *cille*, that is to say, the *dove of the cell*, thus adding to his primitive

---

* Adamnan, who was born in 624, must have written the biography of St Columba between 690 and 703, a period at which he gave up the liturgical traditions of the Scots and the direction of the Monastery of Iona to settle near the Anglo-Saxon king of Northumbria, Aldfrid.

name a special designation, intended to recall either the essentially monastic character of the saint, or the great number of communities founded and governed by him. He was a scion of one of those great Irish races, of whom it is literally true to say that they lose themselves in the night of ages, but which have retained to our own day, thanks to the tenacious attachment of the Irish people to their national recollections, through all the vicissitudes of conquest, persecution, and exile, a rank more patriotic and popular than that of mere nobility or aristocratic lineage. This was the great race of the Nialls or O'Donnells (*clan Domhnaill*), which, native to and master of all the north-western part of the island (the modern counties of Tyrconnell, Tyrone, and Donegal), held sovereign sway in Hibernia and Caledonia, over the two shores of the Scottish sea, during the sixth century. Almost without interruption, up to 1168, kings, springing from its different branches, exercised in Ireland the supreme monarchy—that is to say, a sort of primacy over the provincial kings, which has been compared to that of metropolitan over bishops, but which rather recalls the feudal sovereignty of the Salic emperors, or of the kings of the family of Capet over the great vassals of Germany and France, in the eleventh and twelfth centuries. Nothing could be more unsettled or stormy than the exercise of this sovereignty. It was incessantly disputed by some vassal king, who generally succeeded by force of arms in robbing the supreme monarch of his crown and his life, and replacing him upon the throne of Tara, with a tolerable certainty of being himself similarly treated by the son of the dethroned prince. Besides, the right of succession in Ireland was not regulated by the law of primogeniture. According to the custom known under the name of *Tanistry*, the eldest blood-relation succeeded every deceased prince or chief, and the brother in consequence preceded the son in the order of succession.

After the English conquest, the warlike and powerful race of Nialls was able to maintain, by dint of dauntless perseverance, a sort of independent sovereignty in the north-west of Ireland. The names of the O'Neills and O'Donnells, chiefs of its two principal branches, and too often at war with each other, are to be found on every page of the annals of unhappy Ireland. After the Reformation, when religious persecution had come in to aggravate all the evils of the conquest, these two houses supplied their indignant and unsubdued country with a succession of heroic soldiers who struggled to the death against the perfidious and sanguinary despotism of the Tudors and Stuarts. Ten centuries passed in such desperate struggles have not weakened the traditions which link the saint whose history we are about to tell to those champions of an ancient faith and an outraged country. Even under the reign of Elizabeth, the vassals of young

Hugh O'Donnell, called Red Hugh, so renowned in the poetical records and popular traditions of Erin, and the most dangerous antagonist of English tyranny, recognised in him the hero indicated in the prophetic songs of Columb-kill, and thus placed his glory and that of his ancestors under the wing of the *Dove of the cells*, as under a patronage at once domestic and celestial.

The father of Columba was descended from one of the eight sons of the great king Niall, of the Nine Hostages, who was supreme monarch of all Ireland from 379 to 405, at the period when Patrick was brought to the island as a slave. Consequently he sprang from a race which had reigned in Ireland for six centuries; and in virtue of the ordinary law of succession, might himself have been called to the throne. His mother belonged to a reigning family in Leinster, one of the four subordinate kingdoms of the island. He was born at Gartan, in one of the wildest districts of the present county of Donegal—where the slab of stone upon which his mother lay at the moment of his birth is still shown. He who passes a night upon that stone is cured for ever from the pangs of nostalgia, and will never be consumed, while absent or an exile, by a too passionate love for his country. Such at least is the belief of the poor Irish emigrants, who flock thither at the moment when they are about to abandon the confiscated and ravaged soil of their country to seek their living in America, moved by a touching recollection of the great missionary who gave up his native land for the love of God and human souls.

Before his birth, his mother had a dream, which posterity has accepted as a graceful and poetical symbol of her son's career. An angel appeared to her, bringing her a veil covered with flowers of wonderful beauty, and the sweetest variety of colours; immediately after she saw the veil carried away by the wind, and rolling out as it fled over plains, woods, and mountains: then the angel said to her, "Thou art about to become the mother of a son, who shall blossom for heaven, who shall be reckoned among the prophets of God, and who shall lead numberless souls to the heavenly country." This spiritual power, this privilege of leading souls to heaven, was recognised by the Irish people, converted by St Patrick, as the greatest glory which its princes and great men could gain.

The Irish legends, which are always distinguished, even amidst the wildest vagaries of fancy, by a high and pure morality, linger lovingly upon the childhood and youth of the predestined saint. They tell us how, confided in the first place to the care of the priest who had baptised him, and who gave him the first rudiments of literary education, he was accustomed from his earliest years to the heavenly visions which were to occupy so large a place in his life. His guardian angel often appeared to him; and the child asked if all the angels in heaven were as young and shining as he. A little later Columba was invited by the same angel to choose among all the virtues those which he would like best to possess. "I choose," said the youth, "chastity and wisdom;" and immediately three young girls of wonderful beauty, but foreign air, appeared to him, and threw themselves on his neck to embrace him. The pious youth frowned, and repulsed them with indignation. "What!" they said; "then thou dost not know us?" "No, not the least in the world." "We are three sisters whom our father gives to thee to be thy brides." "Who, then, is your father?" "Our father is God, he is Jesus Christ, the Lord and Saviour of the world." "Ah, you have, indeed, an illustrious father. But what are your names?" "Our names are Virginity, Wisdom, and Prophecy; and we come to leave thee no more, to love thee with an incorruptible love."

From the house of the priest, Columba passed into the great monastic schools, which were not only a nursery for the clergy of the Irish Church, but where also young laymen of all conditions were educated. Columba, like many others, there learned to make his first steps in that monastic life to which he had been drawn by the call of God. He devoted himself not only to study and prayer, but also to the manual toil then inseparable, in Ireland and everywhere else, from a religious profession. Like all his young companions, he had to grind overnight the corn for the next day's food: but when his turn came, it was so well and quickly done that his companions suspected him of having been assisted by an angel. The royal birth of Columba procured him several distinctions in the schools which were not always to the satisfaction of his comrades. One of the latter, named Kieran, who was also destined to fill a great place in Scotic legend, became indignant at the ascendancy of Columba; but while the two students disputed, a celestial messenger came to Kieran and placed before him an auger, a plane, and an axe, saying, "Look at these tools, and recollect that these are all thou hast sacrificed for God, since thy father was only a carpenter; but Columba has sacrificed the sceptre of Ireland, which might have come to him by right of his birth and the grandeur of his race."

We learn from authentic documents that Columba completed his monastic life under the direction of two holy abbots, both bearing the name of Finnian. The first, who was also a bishop, ordained him deacon, but seems to have had him for a shorter time under his authority than the second Finnian, who, himself trained by a disciple of St Patrick, had long lived in Cambria, near St David. Columbia's first steps in life are thus connected with the two great monastic apostles of Ireland and Cambria, the patriarchs of the two Celtic races which up to this time had shown the most entire fidelity to the Christian faith, and the greatest predilection for monastic life. The Abbot Finnian, who ordained Columba priest, ruled at Clonard the monastery which he had founded, and of which we have already spoken—one of those immense conventual establishments which were to be found nowhere but among the Celts, and which recalled to recollection the monastic towns of the Thebaïd. He had made of his monastery one great school, which was filled with the Irish youth, then, as always, consumed by a thirst for religious instruction; and we again find here the favourite number, so often repeated by Celtic tradition, of three thousand pupils, all eager to receive the instructions of him who was called the Master of Saints.

While Columba studied at Clonard, being still only a deacon, an incident took place which has been proved by authentic testimony, and which fixed the general attention upon him by giving a first evidence of his supernatural and prophetic intuition. An old Christian bard (the bards were not all Christians), named Gemmaïn, had come to live near the Abbot Finnian, asking from him, in exchange for his poetry, the secret of fertilising the soil. Columba, who continued all his life a passionate admirer of the traditionary poetry of his nation, determined to join the school of the bard, and to share his labours and studies. The two were reading together out of doors, at a little distance from each other, when a young girl appeared in the distance pursued by a robber. At the sight of the old man the young fugitive made for him with all her remaining strength, hoping, no doubt, to find safety in the authority exercised throughout Ireland by the national poets. Gemmaïn, in great trouble, called his pupil to his aid to defend the unfortunate child, who was trying to hide herself under their long robes when her pursuer reached the spot. Without taking any notice of her defenders, he struck her in the neck with his lance, and was making off, leaving her dead at their feet. The horrified old man turned to Columba. "How long," he said, "will God leave unpunished this crime which dishonours us?" "For this moment only," said Columba, "not longer: at this very hour, when the soul of this innocent creature ascends to heaven, the soul of the murderer shall go down to hell." At the instant, like Ananias at the words of Peter, the assassin fell dead. The news of this sudden punishment, the story goes, went over all Ireland, and spread the fame of the young Columba far and wide.

It is easy to perceive, by the importance of the monastic establishments which he had brought into being even before he had attained the age of manhood, that his influence must have been as precocious as it was considerable. Apart from the virtues of which his after life afforded so many examples, it may be supposed that his royal birth gave him an irresistible ascendancy in a country where, since the introduction of Christianity, all the early saints, like the principal abbots, belonged to reigning families, and where the influence of blood and the worship of genealogy continue, even to this day, to a degree unknown in other lands. Springing, as has been said, from the same race as the monarch of all Ireland, and consequently himself eligible for the same high office, which was more frequently obtained by election or usurpation than inheritance —nephew or near cousin of the seven monarchs who successively wielded the supreme authority during his life—he was also related by ties of blood to almost all the provincial kings. Thus we see him, during his whole career, treated on a footing of perfect intimacy and equality by all the princes of Ireland and of Caledonia, and exercising a sort of spiritual sway equal or superior to the authority of secular sovereigns.

Before he had reached the age of twenty-five he had presided over the creation of a crowd of monasteries. As many as thirty-seven in Ireland alone recognised him as their founder. The most ancient and important of these foundations were situated, as was formerly that of St Bridget at Kildare, in vast oak-forests, from which they took their name. The first Durrow (*Dair-mach Roboreti campus*), where a cross and well bearing the name of Columba are still to be seen, was erected in the central region called the *umbilical*, or sacred middle of Ireland. The other, Derry (*Doire-chalgaich Roboretum Calgachi*), is situated in the northern part of the island, in Columba's native province, in the hollow of a bay of that sea which separates Ireland from Scotland. After having long been the seat of a great and rich Catholic bishopric, it became, under its modern name of Londonderry, one of the principal centres of English colonisation, and was, in 1690, the bulwark of the Protestant conquest against the powerless efforts of the last of the Stuart kings. But nothing then indicated the possibility of those lamentable changes, nor of the miserable triumphs of inhuman force and wicked persecution.

The young Columba was specially attached to Derry, where he habitually lived. He superintended with care not only the discipline and studies of his community, but external matters, even so far as to watch over the preservation of the neighbouring forest. He would never permit an oak to be cut down. Those which fell by natural decay, or were struck down by the wind, were alone made use of for the fire which was lighted on the arrival of strangers, or distributed to the neighbouring poor. The poor had a first right, in Ireland, as everywhere else, to the goods of the monks; and the Monastery of Derry fed a hundred applicants every day with methodical regularity.

At a more advanced age our saint gave vent to his tenderness for his monastic creations in songs, an echo of which has come down to us. The text of these songs, such as has been preserved, is probably later than Columba; but it is written in the oldest Irish dialect, and it expresses, naturally enough, the sentiments of the founder and his disciples:—

> "Were all the tribute of Scotia* mine,
> From its midland to its borders,
> I would give all for one little cell
> In my beautiful Derry.
> For its peace and for its purity,
> For the white angels that go
> In crowds from one end to the other,
> I love my beautiful Derry.
> For its quietness and its purity,
> For heaven's angels that come and go
> Under every leaf of the oaks,
> I love my beautiful Derry.
>
> My Derry, my fair oak grove,
> My dear little cell and dwelling,
> O God in the heavens above!
> Let him who profanes it be cursed.
> Beloved are Durrow and Derry,
> Beloved is Raphoe the pure,

---

* Let us repeat here that the names of *Scotia, Scotti*, when they occur in works of the seventh to the twelfth century, are almost exclusively applied to Ireland and the Irish, and were extended later to Scotland proper, the north and west of which were peopled by a colony of Irish Scots, only at a later period. From thence comes the name of *Erse, Erysche*, or *Irish*, retained up to our own day, by the Irish dialect, otherwise called Gaelic. In Adamnan, as in Bede, Scotia means Ireland, and modern Scotland is comprehended in the general title of Britannia. At a later period the name of Scotia disappeared in Ireland, and became identified with the country conquered and colonised by the *Scots* in Scotland, like that of *Anglia* in Britain, and *Francia* in Gaul.

> Beloved the fertile Drumhome,
> Beloved are Sords and Kells!
> But sweeter and fairer to me
> The salt sea where the sea-gulls cry;
> When I come to Derry from far,
> It is sweeter and dearer to me—
> Sweeter to me."

Nor was it only his own foundations which he thus celebrated: another poem has been preserved which is attributed to him, and which is dedicated to the glory of the monastic isle of Arran, situated upon the western coast of Ireland, where he had gone to venerate the inhabitants and the sanctuaries:—

> "O Arran, my sun; my heart is in the west with thee. To sleep on thy pure soil is as good as to be buried in the land of St Peter and St Paul. To live within the sound of thy bells is to live in joy. O Arran, my sun, my love is in the west with thee."

These poetic effusions reveal Columba to us under one of his most attractive aspects, as one of the ministrels of the national poetry of Ireland, the intimate union of which with the Catholic faith, and its unconquerable empire over the souls of that generous people, can scarcely be exaggerated. Columba was not only himself a poet, but lived always in great and affectionate sympathy with the bards who, at that time, occupied so high a place in the social and political institutions of Ireland, and who were to be met with everywhere, in the palaces and monasteries, as on the public roads. What he did for this powerful corporation, and how, after having been their brother and friend, he became their protector and saviour, will be seen further on. Let us merely state at present that, himself a great traveller, he received the travelling bards in the different communities where he lived; among others, in that which he had built upon an islet of the lake which the Boyle traverses before it throws itself into the Shannon. He confided to them the care of arranging the monastic and provincial annals, which were to be afterwards deposited in the charter-chest of the community; but, above all, he made them sing for his own pleasure and that of his monks; and the latter reproached him energetically if he permitted one of those wandering poets to depart without having asked to hear some of his chants, accompanied by his harp.

The monk Columba was, then, a poet. After Ossian and his glorious compeer of the Vosges, he opens the series of two hundred Irish poets, whose memories and names, in default of their works, have remained dear to Ireland. He wrote his verses not only in Latin, but also and more frequently in Irish. Only three of his Latin poems survive; but two centuries ago eleven of his Irish poems were still in existence, which have not all perished, and the most authentic of which is dedicated to the glory of St Bridget, the virgin slave, patroness of Ireland and foundress of female religious life in the Isle of Saints. She was still living when Columba was born. Through the obscure and halting efforts of this infantine poetry, some tones of sincere and original feeling may yet be disentangled:—

> "Bridget, the good and the virgin,
> Bridget, our torch and our sun,
> Bridget, radiant and unseen,
> May she lead us to the eternal kingdom!
> May Bridget defend us
> Against all the troops of hell,
> And all the adversities of life;
> May she beat them down before us.
> All the ill movements of the flesh,
> This pure virgin whom we love,
> Worthy of honour without end,
> May she extinguish in us.
> Yes, she shall always be our safeguard,
> Dear saint of Lagenia;
> After Patrick she comes the first,
> The pillar of the land,
> Glorious among all glories,
> Queen among all queens.
> When old age comes upon us,
> May she be to us as the shirt of hair,
> May she fill us with her grace,
> May Bridget protect us."

It seems thus apparent that Columba was as much a bard as a monk during the first part of his life; he had the vagabond inclination, the ardent, agitated, even quarrelsome character of the race. Like most Irish saints and even monks whom history has kept in mind, he had a passionate love for travelling; and to that passion he added another which brought him more than one misadventure. Books, which were less rare in Ireland than everywhere else, were nevertheless much sought after, and guarded with jealous care in the monastic libraries, which were their sole depositories. Not only an excessive value was put upon them, but they were even supposed to possess the emotions and almost the passions of living beings. Columba had a passion for fine manuscripts, and one of his biographers attributes to him the laborious feat of having transcribed with his own hand three hundred copies of the Gospel or of the Psalter. He went everywhere in search of volumes which he could borrow or copy, often experiencing refusals which he resented bitterly. There was then in Ossory, in the south-west, a holy recluse, very learned, doctor in laws and in philosophy, named Longarad *with the white legs*, because in walking barefoot his legs, which were covered with white hair, were visible. Columba, having gone to visit him, asked leave to examine his books. The old man gave a direct refusal; then Columba burst forth in denunciations—" May thy books no longer do thee any good, neither to thee nor to those who come after thee, since thou takest occasion by them to show thy inhospitality." This curse was heard, according to the legend. As soon as old Longarad died his books became unintelligible. They still exist, says an author of the ninth century, but no man can read them. The legend adds that in all the schools of Ireland, and even in Columba's own cell, the leathern satchels in which the monks and students carried their books, unhooked themselves from the wall and fell to the ground on the day of the old philosopher's death.

A similar narrative, more authentic but not less singular, serves as an introduction to the decisive event which changed the destiny of Columba, and transformed him from a wandering poet and ardent bookworm into a missionary and apostle. While visiting his ancient master, Finnian, our saint found means to make a clandestine and hurried copy of the abbot's Psalter, by shutting himself up at night in the church where the Psalter was deposited, lighting his nocturnal work, as happened to I know not what Spanish saint, by the light which escaped from his left hand while he wrote with the right. The Abbot Finnian discovered what was going on by means of a curious wanderer, who, attracted by that singular light, looked in through the keyhole, and while his face was pressed against the door had his eye suddenly torn out by a crane, one of those familiar birds who were permitted by the Irish monks to seek a home in their churches. Indignant at what he thought a theft, Finnian claimed the copy when it was finished, on the ground that a copy made without permission ought to belong to the master of the original, seeing that the transcription is the son of the original book. Columba refused to give up his work, and the question was referred to the king in his palace at Tara.

King Diarmid or Dermott, supreme monarch of Ireland, was, like Columba, descended from the great King Niall, but by another son than he whose great-grandson Columba was. He lived, like all the princes of his country, in a close union with the Church, which was represented in Ireland, more completely than anywhere else, by the monastic order. Exiled and persecuted in his youth, he had found refuge in an island, situated in one of those lakes which interrupt the course of the Shannon, the chief river of Ireland, and had there formed a friendship with a holy monk called Kieran, who was no other than the son of the carpenter, the jealous comrade of Columba at the monastic school of Clonard, but since that time his generous rival in knowledge and in austerity. Upon the still solitary bank of the river the two friends had planned the foundation of a monastery, which, owing to the marshy nature of the soil, had to be built upon piles. "Plant with me the first stake," the monk said to the exiled prince, " putting your hand under mine; and soon that hand shall be over all the men of Erin;" and it happened that Diarmid was very shortly after called to the throne. He immediately used his new power to endow richly the monastery which was rendered doubly dear to him by the recollection of his exile and of his friend. This sanctuary became, under the name of Clonmacnoise, one of the greatest monasteries and most frequented schools of Ireland, and even of Western Europe. It was so rich in possessions and even in dependent communities, daughters or vassals of its hierarchical authority, that, according to a popular saying, half of Ireland was contained within the enclosure of Clonmacnoise. This enclosure actually contained nine churches, with two round towers; the kings and lords of the two banks of the Shannon had their burying-place there for a thousand years, upon a green height which overlooks the marshy banks of the river. The sadly picturesque ruins may still be seen, and among them a stone cross, over which the prince and the abbot, holding between them the stake consecrated by the legend, are roughly sculptured.

This king might accordingly be regarded as a competent judge in a contest at once monastic and literary; he might even have been suspected of partiality for Columba, his kinsman—and yet he pronounced against him. His judgment was given in a rustic phrase which has passed into a proverb in Ireland — *To every cow her calf*, and, consequently, to every book its copy. Columba protested loudly. "It is an unjust sentence," he said, "and I will revenge myself." After this incident a young prince, son of the provincial king of Connaught, who was pursued for having committed an involuntary murder, took refuge with Columba, but was seized and put to death by the king. The irritation of the poet-monk knew no bounds. The ecclesiastical immunity which he enjoyed in his quality of superior and founder of several monasteries ought to have, in his opinion, created a sort of sanctuary around his person, and this immunity had been scandalously violated by the execution of the youth whom he protected. He threatened the king with prompt vengeance. "I will denounce," he said, "to my brethren and my kindred thy wicked judgment, and the violation in my person of the immunity of the Church; they will listen to my complaint, and punish thee sword in hand. Bad king, thou shalt no more see my face in thy province until God, the just Judge, has subdued thy pride. As thou hast humbled me to-day before thy lords and thy friends, God will humble thee on the battle day before thine enemies." Diarmid attempted to retain him by force in the neighbourhood; but, evading the vigilance of his guards, he escaped by night from the court of Tara, and directed his steps to his native province of Tyrconnell. His first stage was Monasterboyce, where he heard from the monks that the king had planted guards on all the ordinary roads to intercept him. He then continued his course by a solitary pathway over the desert hills which lay between him and the north of Ireland; and as he went upon his lonely way, his soul found utterance in a pious song. He fled, chanting the 'Song of Trust,' which has been preserved to us, and which may be reckoned among the most authentic relics of the ancient Irish tongue. We quote from it the following verses:—

"Alone am I on the mountain,
O royal Sun; prosper my path,
And then I shall have nothing to fear.
Were I guarded by six thousand,
Though they might defend my skin,
When the hour of death is fixed,
Were I guarded by six thousand,
In no fortress could I be safe.
Even in a church the wicked are slain,
Even in a isle amidst a lake;
But God's elect are safe
Even in the front of battle.
No man can kill me before my day,
Even had we closed in combat;
And no man can save my life
When the hour of death has come.
My life!
As God pleases let it be;
Nought can be taken from it,
Nought can be added to it:
The lot which God has given
Ere a man dies must be lived out.
He who seeks more, were he a prince,
Shall not a mite obtain.
A guard!
A guard may guide him on his way;
But can they, can they, guard
Against the touch of death? . . .
Forget thy poverty a while;
Let us think of the world's hospitality.
The Son of Mary will prosper thee,
And every guest shall have his share.
Many a time
What is spent returns to the bounteous hand,
And that which is kept back
Not the less has passed away.

> O living God!
> Alas for him who evil works!
> That which he thinks not of comes to him,
> That which he hopes vanishes out of his hand.
> There is no *Sreod** that can tell our fate,
> Nor bird upon the branch,
> Nor trunk of gnarled oak. . . .
> Better is He in whom we trust,
> The King who has made us all,
> Who will not leave me to-night without refuge.
> I adore not the voice of birds,
> Nor chance, nor the love of a son or a wife.
> My Druid is Christ, the Son of God,
> The Son of Mary, the great Abbot,
> The Father, the Son, and the Holy Spirit.
> My lands are with the King of kings;
> My order at Kells and at Moone."

"Thus sang Columba," says the preface to this 'Song of Trust,' "on his lonely journey; and this song will protect him who repeats it while he travels."

Columba arrived safely in his province, and immediately set to work to excite against King Diarmid the numerous and powerful clans of his relatives and friends, who belonged to a branch of the house of Niall distinct from and hostile to that of the reigning monarch. His efforts were crowned with success. The Hy-Nialls of the North armed eagerly against the Hy-Nialls of the South, of whom

---

* An unknown Druidical term, probably meaning some pagan superstition of the same description as the flight of birds and the knots in the trees, mentioned immediately after.

Diarmid was the special chief. They naturally obtained the aid of the king of Connaught, father of the young prince who had been executed. According to other narratives, the struggle was one between the Nialls of the North and the Picts established in the centre of Ireland. But in any case, it was the north and west of Ireland which took arms against the supreme king. Diarmid marched to meet them, and they met in battle at Cool-Drewny, or Cul-Dreimhne, upon the borders of Ultonia and Connacia. He was completely beaten, and obliged to take refuge at Tara. The victory was due, according to the annalist Tighernach, to the prayers and songs of Columba, who had fasted and prayed with all his might to obtain from Heaven the punishment of the royal insolence, and who, besides, was present at the battle, and took upon himself before all men the responsibility of the bloodshed.

As for the manuscript which had been the object of this strange conflict of copyright elevated into a civil war, it was afterwards venerated as a kind of national, military, and religious palladium. Under the name of *Cathac*, or *Fighter*, the Latin Psalter transcribed by Columba, enshrined in a sort of portable altar, became the national relic of the O'Donnell clan. For more than a thousand years it was carried with them to battle as a pledge of victory, on the condition of being supported upon the breast of a clerk pure from all mortal sin. It has escaped as by miracle from the ravages of which Ireland has been the victim, and exists still, to the great joy of all learned Irish patriots.

Columba, though victor, had soon to undergo the double reaction of personal remorse and the condemnation of many pious souls. The latter punishment was the first to be felt. He was accused, by a synod convoked in the centre of the royal domain at Teilte, of having occasioned the shedding of Christian blood, and sentence of excommunication was in his absence pronounced against him. Perhaps this accusation was not entirely confined to the war which had been raised on account of the copied Psalter. His excitable and vindictive character, and, above all, his passionate attachment to his relatives, and the violent part which he took in their domestic disputes and in their continually recurring rivalries, had engaged him in other struggles, the date of which is perhaps later than that of his first departure from Ireland, but the responsibility of which is formally imputed to him by various authorities, and which also ended in bloody battles.

Columba was not a man to draw back before his accusers and judges. He presented himself before the synod which had struck without hearing him. He found a defender there in the famous Abbot Brendan, the founder of the Monastery of Birr. When Columba made his appearance, this abbot rose, went up to him, and embraced him. "How can you give the kiss of peace to an excommunicated man?" said some of the other members of the synod. "You would do as I have done," he answered, "and you never would have excommunicated him, had you seen what I see—a pillar of fire which goes before him, and the angels that accompany him. I dare not disdain a man predestined by God to be the guide of an entire people to eternal life." Thanks to the intervention of Brendan, or to some other motive not mentioned, the sentence of excommunication was withdrawn; but Columba was charged to win to Christ by his preaching as many pagan souls as the number of Christians who had fallen in the battle of Cool-Drewny.

It was then that his soul seems first to have been troubled, and that remorse planted in it the germs at once of a startling conversion and of his future apostolic mission. Sheltered as he was from all vengeance or secular penalties, he must have felt himself struck so much the more by the ecclesiastical judgment pronounced against him. Various legends reveal him to us at this crisis of his life, wandering long from solitude to solitude, and from monastery to monastery, seeking out holy monks, masters of penitence and Christian virtue, and asking them anxiously what he should do to obtain the pardon of God for the murder of so many victims. One of these, Froëch, who had long been his friend, reproached him with affectionate severity for having been the instigator of that murderous fight. "It was not I who caused it," said Columba with animation; "it was the unjust judgment of King Diarmid—it was his violation of ecclesiastical immunity which did it all." "A monk," answered the solitary, "would have done better to bear the injury with patience than to avenge it with arms in his hands." "Be it so," said Columba; "but it is hard for a man unjustly provoked to restrain his heart and to sacrifice justice."

He was more humble with Abban, another famous monk of the time, founder of many religious houses, one of which was called the *Cell of Tears*, because the special grace of weeping for sin was obtained there. This gentle and courageous soldier of Christ was specially distinguished by his zeal against the fighting men and disturbers of the public peace. He had been seen to throw himself between two chiefs at the moment when their lances were crossed at each other's breasts; and on another occasion had gone alone and unarmed to meet one of the most formidable rievers of the island, who was still a pagan and a member of a sovereign family, had made his arms drop from his hands, and had changed first into a Christian and then into a monk the royal robber, whose great-grandson has recorded this incident. When Columba went to Abban, he said, "I come to beseech thee to pray for the souls of all those who have perished in the late war, which I raised for the honour of the Church. I know they will obtain grace by thy intercession, and I conjure thee to ask what is the will of God in respect to them from the angel who talks with thee every day." The aged solitary, without reproaching Columba, resisted his entreaties for some time, by reason of his great modesty, but ended by consenting; and after having prayed, gave him the assurance that these souls enjoyed eternal repose.

Columba, thus reassured as to the fate of the victims of his rage, had still to be enlightened in respect to his own duty. He found the light which he sought from a holy monk called Molaise, famed for his studies of Holy Scripture, who had already been his confessor, and whose ruined monastery is still visible in Innishmurry, on the coast of Sligo, one of the isles of the Atlantic. This severe hermit confirmed the decision of the synod; but to the obligation of converting to the Christian faith an equal number of pagans as there were of Christians killed in the civil war he added a new condition, which bore cruelly upon a soul so passionately attached to country and kindred. The confessor condemned his penitent to perpetual exile from Ireland. Columba bowed to this sentence with sad resignation—"What you have commanded," he said, "shall be done."

He announced his future fate in the first place to his relations, the warlike Nialls of Tyrconnell. "An angel has taught me that I must leave Ireland and remain in exile as long as I live, because of all those whom you slew in the last battle, which you fought on my account, and also in others which you know of." It is not recorded that any among his kindred attempted to hold him back; but when he acquainted his disciples with his intended emigration, twelve among them decided to follow him. The most ardent of all was a young monk called Mochonna, son of the provincial king of Ulster. In vain Columba represented to him that he ought not to abandon his parents and native soil. "It is thou," answered the young man, "who art my father, the Church is my mother, and my country is where I can gather the largest harvest for Christ." Then, in order to render all resistance impossible, he made a solemn vow aloud to leave his country and follow Columba—"I swear to follow thee wherever thou goest, until thou hast led me to Christ, to whom thou hast consecrated me." It was thus, says his historian, that he forced himself rather than offered himself as a companion to the great exile in the course of his apostolical career among the Picts—and he had no more active or devoted auxiliary.

Columba accepted, though not without sadness, as has been seen, the sentence of his friend. He dedicated the rest of his life to the expiation of his faults by a voluntary exile, and by preaching the faith to the heathen. Up to this time we have had difficulty in disentangling the principal events of the first forty years of his life from a maze of confused and contradictory narratives. We have followed what has seemed to us the most probable account, and one most calculated to throw light upon the character of the saint, his people, and his country. Henceforward we shall find a surer guide in Adamnan, who only touches very slightly upon the first half of his hero's life, and who, with an apparent contempt for the unanimous testimony of Irish witnesses, while agreeing that the departure of the saint took place after the battle in which the King of Ireland had been beaten by Columba's kindred, attributes his departure solely to his desire for the conversion of the heathens of the great neighbouring isle.

CHAPTER II.

Columba an Emigrant in Caledonia—The Holy Isle of Iona.

E who has not seen the islands and gulfs of the western coast of Scotland, and who has not been tossed upon the sombre sea of the Hebrides, can scarcely form any image of it to himself. Nothing can be less seductive at the first glance than that austere and solemn nature, which is picturesque without charm, and grand without grace. The traveller passes sadly through an archipelago of naked and desert islands, sowed, like so many extinct volcanoes, upon the dull and sullen waters, which are sometimes broken by rapid currents and dangerous whirlpools. Except on rare days, when the sun—that pale sun of the North—gives life to these shores, the eye wanders over a vast surface of gloomy sea, broken at intervals by the whitening crest of waves, or by the foamy line of the tide, which

dashes here against long reefs of rock, there against immense cliffs, with a forlorn roar which fills the air. Through the continual fogs and rains of that rude climate may be seen by times the summits of chains of mountains, whose abrupt and naked sides slope to the sea, and whose base is bathed by those cold waves which are kept in constant agitation by the shock of contrary currents, and the tempests of wind which burst from the lakes and narrow ravines farther inland. The melancholy of the landscape is relieved only by that peculiar configuration of the coast, which has been remarked by the ancient authors, and especially by Tacitus—a configuration which exists besides only in Greece and Scandinavia. As in the fiords of Norway, the sea cuts and hollows out the shores of the islands into a host of bays and gulfs, of strange depth, and as narrow as profound. These gulfs take the most varied forms, penetrating by a thousand tortuous folds into the middle of the land, as if to identify themselves with the long and winding lakes of the Highland interior. Numberless peninsulas, terminating in pointed headlands, or summits covered with clouds; isthmuses so narrow as to leave the sea visible at both sides; straits so closely shut between two walls of rock that the eye hesitates to plunge into that gloom; enormous cliffs of basalt or of granite, their sides perforated with rents; caverns, as at Staffa, lofty as churches, flanked through all their length by prismatic columns, through which the waves of the ocean dash with groans; and here and there, in contrast with that wild majesty, perhaps in an island, perhaps upon the shore of the mainland, a sandy beach, a little plain covered with scanty prickling grass; a natural port, capable of sheltering a few frail boats; everywhere, in short, a strangely varied combination of land and sea, but where the sea carries the day, penetrates and dominates everything, as if to affirm her empire, and, as Tacitus has said, "*inseri velut in suo.*"

Such is the present aspect—such must have been, with the addition of the forests which have disappeared, the aspect of those shores when Columba sought them to continue and end his life there. It was from this point that he was to assail the Land of Woods, that unconquerable Caledonia, where the Romans had been obliged to relinquish the idea of establishing themselves, where Christianity hitherto had appeared only to vanish, and which for long seemed to Europe almost outside the boundaries of the world. To Columba was to fall the honour of introducing civilisation into the stony, sterile, and icy *Escosse la Sauvage*, which the imagination of our fathers made the dwelling-place of hunger, and of the prince of demons. Sailing by these distant shores, who could refrain from evoking the holy memory and forgotten glory of the great missionary? It is from him that Scotland has derived that religious spirit which, led astray as it has been since the Reformation, and in spite of its own rigid narrowness, remains still so powerful, so popular, so fruitful, and so free. Half veiled by the misty distance, Columba stands first among those original and touching historical figures to whom Scotland owes the great place she has occupied in the memory and imagination of modern nations, from the noble chivalry of the feudal and Catholic kingdom of the Bruces and Douglases, down to the unparalleled misfortunes of Mary Stuart and Charles Edward, and all the poetic and romantic recollections which the pure and upright genius of Walter Scott has endowed with European fame.

A voluntary exile, at the age of forty-two, from his native island, Columba embarked with his twelve companions in one of those great barks of osier covered with hide which the Celtic nations employed for their navigation. He landed upon a desert island situated on the north of the opening of that series of gulfs and lakes which, extending from the south-west to the north-east, cuts the Caledonian peninsula in two, and which at that period separated the still heathen Picts from the district occupied by the Irish Scots, who were partially Christianised. This isle, which he has made immortal, took from him the name of I-Colm-kill (the island of Columb-kill), but is better known under that of Iona. A legend, suggested by one of our saint's most marked characteristics, asserts that he first landed upon another islet called Oronsay, but that, having climbed a hill near the shore immediately on landing, he found that he could still see Ireland, his beloved country. To see far off that dear soil which he had left for ever, was too hard a trial. He came down from the hill, and immediately took to his boat to seek, farther off, a shore from which he could not see his native land. When he had reached Iona, he climbed the highest point in the island, and, gazing into the distance, found no longer any trace of Ireland upon the horizon. He decided, accordingly, to remain upon this unknown rock. One of those heaps of stones, which are called *cairns* in the Celtic dialect, still marks the spot where Columba made this desiredly unfruitful examination, and has long borne the name of the Cairn of Farewell.*

Nothing could be more sullen and sad than the aspect of this celebrated isle, where not a single tree has been able to resist either the blighting wind or the destroying hand of man. Only three miles in length by two in breadth, flat and low, bordered by grey rocks which scarcely rise above the level of the sea, and overshadowed by the high and sombre peaks of the great island of Mull, it has not even the wild beauty which is conferred upon the neighbouring isles and shores by their basalt cliffs, which are often of prodigious height—or which belongs to the hills, often green and rounded at the summit, whose perpendicular sides are beaten incessantly by those Atlantic waves, which bury

* *Carn cul ri Erin*—literally, *the back turned on Ireland.*

themselves in resounding caverns hollowed by the everlasting labours of that tumultuous sea. Upon the narrow surface of the island white stretches of sand alternate with scanty pastures, a few poor crops, and the turf-moors where the inhabitants find their fuel. Poor as the culture is, it seems everywhere resisted and disputed by the gneiss rocks, which continually crop out, and in some places form an almost inextricable labyrinth. The only attraction possessed by this sombre dwelling-place is the view of the sea, and of the mountains of Mull and the other islands, to the number of twenty or thirty, which may be distinguished from the top of the northern hill of Iona. Among these is Staffa, celebrated for the grotto of Fingal, which has been known only for about a century, and which, in the time of Columba, moaned and murmured in its solitary and unknown majesty, in the midst of that Hebridean archipelago which is at present haunted by so many curious admirers of the Highland shores and ruined feudal castles, which the great bard of our century has enshrined in the glory of his verse.

The bay where Columba landed is still called the *bay of the osier bark, Port' a Churraich;* and a long mound is pointed out to strangers as representing the exact size of his boat, which was sixty feet long. The emigrant did not remain in this bay, which is situated in the middle of the isle; he went higher up, and, to find a little shelter from the great sea winds, chose for his habitation the eastern shore, opposite the large island of Mull, which is separated from Iona only by a narrow channel of a mile in breadth, and whose highest mountains, situated more to the east, approach and almost identify themselves with the mountain-tops of Morven, which are continually veiled with clouds. It was there that the emigrants built their huts of branches, for the island was not then, as now, destitute of wood. When Columba had made up his mind to construct for himself and his people a settled establishment, the buildings of the new-born monastery were of the greatest simplicity. As in all Celtic constructions, walls of withes or branches, supported upon long wooden props, formed the principal element in their architecture. Climbing plants, especially ivy, interlacing itself in the interstices of the branches, at once ornamented and consolidated the modest shelter of the missionaries. The Irish built scarcely any churches of stone, and retained, up to the twelfth century, as St Bernard testifies, the habit of building their churches of wood. But it was not for some years after their first establishment that the monks of Iona permitted themselves the luxury of a wooden church; and when they did so, great oaks, such as the sterile and wind-beaten soil of their islet could not produce, had to be brought for its construction from the neighbouring shore.

Thus the monastic capital of Scotland, and the centre of Christian civilisation in the north of Great Britain, came into being thirteen centuries ago.

Some ruins of a much later date than the days of Columba, though still very ancient, mingled among a few cottages scattered on the shore, still point out the site.

"We were now treading," said, in the eighteenth century, the celebrated Johnson, who was the first to recall the attention of the British public to this profaned sanctuary—"we were now treading that illustrious island which was once the luminary of the Caledonian regions, whence savage clans and roving barbarians derived the benefits of knowledge, and the blessings of religion. To abstract the mind from all local emotion would be impossible, if it were endeavoured, and would be foolish, if it were possible. Whatever withdraws us from the power of our senses, whatever makes the past, the distant, or the future predominate over the present, advances us in the dignity of thinking beings. Far from me, and from my friends, be such frigid philosophy as may conduct us indifferent and unmoved over any ground which has been dignified by wisdom, bravery, or virtue. That man is little to be envied whose patriotism would not gain force upon the plain of Marathon, or whose piety would not grow warmer among the ruins of Iona!"

Columba, who had been initiated into classic recollections, like all the monks of his time, had no doubt heard of Marathon; but certainly it could never have occurred to him that a day would come in which a descendant of the race he came to save should place his humble shelter in the same rank with the most glorious battle-field of Hellenic history.

Far from having any prevision of the glory of Iona, his soul was still swayed by a sentiment which never abandoned him — regret for his lost country. All his life he retained for Ireland the passionate tenderness of an exile, a love which displayed itself in the songs which have been preserved to us, and which date perhaps from the first moments of his exile. It is possible that their authenticity is not altogether beyond dispute; and that, like the poetic lamentations given forth by Fortunatus in the name of St Radegund, they were composed by his disciples and contemporaries. But they have been too long repeated as his, and depict too well what must have passed in his heart, to permit us to neglect them. " Death in faultless Ireland is better than life without end in Albyn." After this cry of despair follow strains more plaintive and submissive. In one of his elegies he laments that he can no longer sail on the lakes and bays of his native island, nor hear the song of the swans, with his friend Comgall. He laments above all to have been driven from Erin by his own fault, and because of the blood shed in his battles. He envies his friend Cormac, who can go back to his dear monastery at Durrow, and hear the wind sigh among the oaks, and the song of the blackbird and cuckoo. As for Columba, all is dear to him in Ireland *except the princes who reign there.* This last particular shows the persistence of his political rancour. No trace of this feeling, however, remains in a still more characteristic poem, which must have been confided to some traveller as a message from the exile of Iona to his country. In this he celebrates, as always, the delight of voyaging round the coast of Ireland, and the beauty of its cliffs and beach. But, above all, he mourns over his exile :—

"What joy to fly upon the white-crested sea, and to watch the waves break upon the Irish shore! what joy to row the little bark, and land among the whitening foam upon the Irish shore! Ah! how my boat would fly if its prow were turned to my Irish oak-grove! But the noble sea now carries me only to Albyn,[*] the land of ravens. My foot is in my little boat, but my sad heart ever bleeds. There is a grey eye which ever turns to Erin; but never in this life shall it see Erin, nor her sons, nor her daughters. From the high prow I look over the sea, and great tears are in my grey eye when I turn to Erin—to Erin, where the songs of the birds are so sweet, and where the clerks sing like the birds; where the young are so gentle, and the old so wise; where the great men are so noble to look

[*] Albania was the original name of the country which the Romans called Caledonia, and which is now known as Scotland.

at, and the women so fair to wed. Young traveller, carry my sorrows with thee, carry them to Comgall of eternal life. Noble youth, take my prayer with thee, and my blessing; one part for Ireland—seven times may she be blessed! and the other for Albyn. Carry my blessing across the sea—carry it to the west. My heart is broken in my breast: if death comes to me suddenly, it will be because of the great love I bear to the Gael."

But it was not only in these elegies, repeated and perhaps retouched by Irish bards and monks, but at each instant of his life, in season and out of season, that this love and passionate longing for his native country burst forth in words and in musings; the narratives of his most trustworthy biographers are full of it. The most severe penance which he could imagine for the guiltiest sinners who came to confess to him, was to impose upon them the same fate which he had voluntarily inflicted upon himself—never to set foot again upon Irish soil. But when, instead of forbidding to sinners all access to that beloved isle, he had to smother his envy of those who had the right and happiness to go there at their pleasure, he dared scarcely trust himself to name its name; and when speaking to his guests, or to the monks who were to return to Ireland, he could only say to them, "You will return to the country that you love."

This melancholy patriotism never faded out of his heart, and was evidenced much later in his life by an incident which shows an obstinate regret for his lost Ireland, along with a tender and careful solicitude for all the creatures of God. One morning he called one of the monks and said to him, "Go and seat thyself by the sea, upon the western bank of the island; there thou wilt see arrive from the north of Ireland and fall at thy feet a poor travelling stork, long beaten by the winds and exhausted by fatigue. Take her up with pity, feed her and watch her for three days; after three days' rest, when she is refreshed and strengthened, she will no longer wish to prolong her exile among us —she will fly to sweet Ireland, her dear country where she was born. I bid thee care for her thus, because she comes from the land where I, too, was born." Everything happened as he had said and ordered. The evening of the day on which the monk had received the poor traveller, as he returned to the monastery, Columba, asking him no questions, said to him, "God bless thee, my dear child, thou hast cared for the exile; in three days thou shalt see her return to her country." And, in fact, at the time mentioned the stork rose from the ground in her host's presence, and, after having sought her way for a moment in the air, directed her flight across the sea, straight upon Ireland. The sailors of the Hebrides all know and tell this tale; and I love to think that among all my readers there is not one who would not fain have repeated or deserved Columba's blessing.

CHAPTER III.

The Apostolate of Columba among the Scots and Picts.

HOWEVER bitter the sadness might be with which exile filled the heart of Columba, it did not for a moment turn him from his work of expiation. As soon as he had installed himself with his companions in that desert isle, from whence the Christian faith and monastic life were about to radiate over the north of Great Britain, a gradual and almost complete transformation became apparent in him. Without giving up the lovable peculiarities of his character and race, he gradually became a model for penitents, and at the same time for confessors and preachers. Without ceasing to maintain an authority which was to increase with years, and which does not seem ever to have been disputed, over the monasteries which he had founded in Ireland, he applied himself at once to establish, on the double basis of manual and intellectual labour, the new insular community which was to be the centre of his future activity. Then he proceeded to unite himself in friendly relations with the inhabitants of the neighbouring districts, whom it was needful to evangelise or confirm in the faith, before thinking of carrying the light of the Gospel further off to the north. He prepared himself for this grand mission by miracles of fervour and austerity, as well as humble charity, to the great profit in the first place of his own monks, and afterwards of the many visitors who came, whether from Ireland or from the Caledonian shores, to seek at his side the healing or the consolation of penitence.

This man, whom we have seen so passionate, so irritable, so warlike and vindictive, became little by little the most gentle, the humblest, the most tender of friends and fathers. It was he, the great head of the Caledonian Church, who, kneeling before the strangers who came to Iona, or before the monks returning from their work, took off their shoes, washed their feet, and after having washed them respectfully kissed them. But charity was still stronger than humility in that transfigured soul. No necessity, spiritual or temporal, found him indifferent. He devoted himself to the solace of all infirmities, all misery, and pain, weeping often over those who did not weep for themselves. These tears became the most eloquent part of his preaching, the means which he employed most willingly to subdue inveterate sinners, to arrest the criminal on the brink of the abyss, to appease and soften and change those wild and savage but simple and straightforward souls, whom God had given him to subdue.

In the midst of the new community Columba inhabited, instead of a cell, a sort of hut built of planks, and placed upon the most elevated spot within the monastic enclosure. Up to the age of seventy-six he slept there upon the hard floor, with no pillow but a stone. This hut was at once his study and his oratory. It was there that he gave himself up to those prolonged prayers which excited the admiration and almost the alarm of his disciples. It was there that he returned after sharing the outdoor labour of his monks, like the least among them, to consecrate the rest of his time to the study of Holy Scripture and the transcription of the sacred text. The work of transcription remained until his last day the occupation of his old age as it had been the passion of his youth; it had such an attraction for him, and seemed to him so essential to a knowledge of the truth, that, as we have already said, three hundred copies of the Holy Gospels, copied by his own hand, have been attributed to him. It was in the same hut that he received with unwearied patience the numerous and sometimes importunate visitors who soon flowed to him, and of whom sometimes he complained gently—as of that indiscreet stranger, who, desirous of embracing him, awkwardly overturned his ink upon the border of his robe. These importunate guests did not come out of simple curiosity; they were most commonly penitent or fervid Christians, who, informed by the fishermen and inhabitants of the neighbouring isles of the establishment of the Irish monk, who was already famous in his own country, and attracted by the growing renown of his virtues, came from Ireland, from the north and south of Britain, and even from the midst of the still heathen Saxons, to save their souls and gain heaven under the direction of a man of God.

Far from making efforts to attract or lightly admitting these neophytes, nothing in his life is more clearly established than the scrupulous severity with which he examined into all vocations, and into the admission of penitents. He feared nothing so much as that the monastic frock might serve as a shelter for criminals who sought in the cloister not only a place of penitence and expiation, but a shelter from human justice. On occasion he even blamed the too great facility of his friends and disciples. One of the latter, Finchan, had founded upon Eigg, another Hebridean island, to the north of Iona, near Skye, a community resembling that of Iona, and possibly dependent upon it : he had there admitted to clerical orders, and even to the priesthood, a prince of the clan of Picts established in Ireland,

Aëdh or Aïdus, called the Black, a violent and bloodthirsty man, who had assassinated Diarmid, the king of Ireland. It was this king, as will be remembered, who pronounced the unjust sentence which drove Columba frantic, and was the occasion of all his faults and misfortunes. The abbot of Iona was not the less on this account indignant at the weakness of his friend. "The hand which Finchan has laid, in the face of all justice and ecclesiastical law, upon the head of this son of perdition," said Columba, "shall rot and fall off, and be buried before the body to which it is attached. As for the false priest, the assassin, he shall himself be assassinated." This double prophecy was accomplished.

Let us lend an ear to the following dialogue which Columba held with one of those who sought shelter under his discipline. It will explain the moral and spiritual condition of that age better than many commentaries, and will, besides, show the wonderful influence which Columba, penitent and exiled in the depths of his distant island, exercised over all Ireland. It was one day announced to him that a stranger had just landed from Ireland, and Columba went to meet him in the house reserved for guests, to talk to him in private, and question him as to his dwelling-place, his family, and the cause of his journey. The stranger told him that he had undertaken this painful voyage in order, under the monastic habit and in exile, to expiate his sins. Columba, desirous of trying the reality of his penitence, drew a most repulsive picture of the hardship and difficult obligations of the new life. "I am ready," said the stranger, "to submit to the most cruel and humiliating conditions that thou canst command me." And after having made confession, he swore, still upon his knees, to accomplish all the requirements of penitence. "It is well," said the abbot; "now rise from thy knees, seat thyself, and listen: you must first do penance for seven years in the neighbouring island of Tiree, after which I will see you again." "But," said the penitent, still agitated by remorse, "how can I expiate a perjury of which I have not yet spoken? Before I left my own country I killed a poor man. I was about to suffer the punishment of death for that crime, and I was already in irons, when one of my relations, who is very rich, delivered me by paying the composition demanded. I swore that I would serve him all the rest of my life; but after some days of service I abandoned him, and here I am, notwithstanding my oath." Upon this the saint added that he would only be admitted to the paschal communion after seven years of penitence. When these were completed, Columba, after having given him the communion with his own hand, sent him back to Ireland to his patron, carrying a sword with an ivory handle for his ransom. The patron, however, moved by the entreaties of his wife, gave the penitent his pardon without ransom. "Why should we accept the price sent to us by the holy

Columba? We are not worthy of it. The request of such an intercessor should be granted freely. His blessing will do more for us than any ransom." And immediately he detached the girdle from his waist, which was the ordinary formula in Ireland for the manumission of captives or slaves. Columba had besides commanded his penitent to remain with his old father and mother until he had rendered to them the last services. This accomplished, his brothers let him go, saying, "Far be it from us to detain a man who has laboured for seven years for the salvation of his soul with the holy Columba." He then returned to Iona, bringing with him the sword which was to have been his ransom. "Henceforward thou shalt be called Libran, for thou art free, and emancipated from all ties," said Columba; and he immediately admitted him to take the monastic vows. But when he was commanded to return to Tiree, to end his life at a distance from Columba, poor Libran, who up to this moment had been so docile, fell on his knees and wept bitterly. Columba, touched by his despair, comforted him as best he could, without, however, altering his sentence. "Thou shalt live far from me, but thou shalt die in one of my monasteries, and thou shalt rise again with my monks, and have part with them in heaven," said the abbot. Such was the history of Libran, called Libran of the Rushes, because he had passed many years in gathering rushes —the years probably of his penitence.

This doctor, learned in penitence, became day by day more gifted in the great art of ruling souls ; and, with a hand as prudent as vigorous, raised up on one side the wounded and troubled conscience, while, on the other, he unveiled the false monks and false penitents. To a certain monk, who, in despair at having yielded during a journey to the temptations of a woman, rushed from confessor to confessor without ever finding himself sufficiently repentant or sufficiently punished, he restored peace and confidence, by showing him that his despair was nothing but an infernal hallucination, and by inflicting upon him a penance hard enough to convince him of the remission of his sin. To another sinner from Ireland, who, guilty of incest and fratricide, had insisted, whether Columba pleased or not, on taking refuge in Iona, he imposed perpetual exile from his native country, and twelve years of penance among the savages of Caledonia, predicting at the same time that the false penitent would perish in consequence of refusing this expiation. Arriving one day in a little community formed by himself in one of the neighbouring islets—Himba, the modern name of which is unknown—and intended to receive the penitents during their time of probation, he gave orders that certain delicacies should be added to their usual repast, and that even the penitents should be permitted to enjoy them. One of the latter, however, more scrupulous than needful, refused to accept the improved fare, even from the hand of the abbot. "Ah!" said Columba, "thou refusest the solace which is offered to thee by thy superior and myself. A day will come when thou shalt again be a robber as thou hast been, and shalt steal, and eat the venison in the forests wherever thou goest." And this prophecy too was fulfilled.

Notwithstanding these precautions, and his apparent severity, the number of neophytes who sought the privilege of living under the rule of Columba increased more and more. Every day, and every minute of the day, the abbot and his companions, in the retirement of their cells, or at their outdoor labours, heard great cries addressed to them from the other side of the narrow strait which separates Iona from the neighbouring island of Mull. These shouts were the understood signal by which those who sought admission to Iona gave notice of their presence, that the boat of the monastery might be sent to carry them over. Among the crowds who crossed in that boat some sought only material help, alms, or medicines; but the greater part sought permission to do penance, and to pass a shorter or longer time in the new monastery, where Columba put their vocation to so many trials. Once only was he known to have at the very moment of their arrival imposed, so to speak, the monastic vows upon two pilgrims, whose virtues and approaching death had been by a supernatural instinct revealed to him.

The narrow enclosure of Iona was soon too small for the increasing crowd, and from this little monastic colony issued in succession a swarm of similar colonies, which went forth to plant new communities, daughters of Iona, in the neighbouring isles, and on the mainland of Caledonia, all of which were under the authority of Columba. Ancient traditions attribute to him the foundation of three hundred monasteries or churches, as many in Caledonia as in Hibernia, a hundred of which were in the islands or upon the sea-shore of the two countries. Modern learning has discovered and registered the existence of ninety churches, whose origin goes back to Columba, and to all or almost all of which, according to the custom of the time, monastic communities must have been attached. Traces of fifty-three of these churches remain still in modern Scotland, unequally divided among the districts inhabited by the two races which then shared Caledonia between them. Thirty-two are in the Western Isles and the country occupied by the Irish-Scots, and the twenty-one others mark the principal stations of the great missionary in the land of the Picts. The most enlightened judges among the Scotch Protestants agree in attributing to the teachings of Columba—to his foundations and his disciples—all the primitive churches, and the very ancient parochial division of Scotland.

But it is time to tell what the population was whose confidence Columba had thus gained, and from which the communities of his monastic family were recruited. The portion of Great Britain which received the name of Caledonia did not include the whole of modern Scotland; it embraced only the districts to the north of the isthmus which separates the Clyde from the Forth, or Glasgow from Edinburgh. All this region to the north and to the east was in the hands of those terrible Picts whom the Romans had been unable to conquer, and who were the terror of the Britons. But to the west and south-west, on the side where Columba landed, he found a colony of his own country and race—that is to say, the Scots of Ireland, who were destined to become the sole masters of Caledonia, and to bestow upon it the name of Scotland. More than half a century before, following in the train of many similar invasions or emigrations, a colony of Irish, or, according to the name then in use, of Scots, belonging to the tribe of Dalriadians, had crossed the sea which separates the north-east coast of Ireland from the north-west of Great Britain, and had established itself—between the Picts of the north and the Britons of the south—in the islands and upon the western coast of Caledonia, north of the mouth of the Clyde, and in the district which has since taken the name of Argyll. The chiefs or kings of this Dalriadian colony, who were destined to become the parent stock of those famous and unfortunate Stuarts who once reigned over both Scotland and England, had at that time strengthened their growing power by the aid of the Niall princes who reigned in the north of Ireland, and to whose family Columba belonged. Columba had also a very close tie of kindred with the Dalriadians themselves, his paternal grandmother having been the daughter of Lorn, the first, or one of the first kings of the colony. He was thus a relation of King Connal, the sixth successor of Lorn, who, at the moment of Columba's arrival, had been for three years the chief of the Scotic emigrants in Caledonia. Iona, where the abbot established himself, was at the northern extremity of the then very limited domain of the Dalriadians, and might be regarded as a dependency of their new state, not less than of that of the Picts, who occupied all the rest of Caledonia. Columba immediately entered into alliance with this prince. He visited him in his residence on the mainland, and obtained from him, in his double title of cousin and countryman, a gift of the uninhabited island where he had just established his community.

These Scots, who had left Ireland after the conversion of the island by St Patrick, were probably Christians, like all the Irish, at least in name; but no certain trace of ecclesiastical organisation or of monastic institutions is visible among them before Columba's arrival at Iona. The apostolate of Ninian and of Palladius does not seem to have produced a durable impression upon them any more than upon the Southern Picts. A new apostolical enterprise by Celtic monks was necessary to renew the work at which the Roman missionaries had laboured a century before. Columba and his disciples neglected no means of fortifying and spreading religion among their countrymen, who were emigrants like themselves. We see him in the narratives of Adamnan administering baptism and the other rites of religion to the people of Scotic race, through whose lands he passed, planting there the first foundations of monastic communities. Many narratives, more or less legendary, indicate that this people, even when Christian, had great need to be instructed, directed, and established in the good way; while at the same time the Dalriadians showed a certain suspicion and doubt of the new apostle of their race, which only yielded to the prolonged influence of his self-devotion and unquestionable virtue.

Columba was still in the flower of his age when he established himself at Iona; he was not more at the most than forty-two. All testimonies agree in celebrating his manly beauty, his remarkable height, his sweet and sonorous voice, the cordiality of his manner, the gracious dignity of his deportment and person. These external advantages, added to the fame of his austerities and the inviolable purity of his life, made a singular and varied impression upon the pagans and the very imperfect Christians of Caledonia. The Dalriadian king put his virtue to the proof by presenting to him his daughter, who was remarkably beautiful, and clothed in the richest ornaments. He asked if the sight of a creature so beautiful and so adorned did not excite some inclination in him. "Without doubt," answered the missionary, "the inclination of the flesh and of nature; but understand well, lord king, that not for all the empire of the world, even could its honours and pleasures be secured to me to the end of time, would I yield to my natural weakness." About the same time, a woman who lived not far from Iona spread for him a more dangerous and subtle snare. The celebrated and handsome exile having inspired her with a violent and guilty passion, she conceived the idea of seducing him, and succeeded in drawing him to her house. But as soon as he understood her design, he addressed to her an exhortation upon death and the last judgment, which he ended by blessing her, and making the sign of the cross. The temptress was thus delivered even from her own temptations. She continued to love him, but with a religious respect. It is added that she herself became a model of holiness.

But it was towards another race, very different from his Scotic countrymen and much less accessible, that Columba felt himself drawn as much by the penance imposed upon him as by the necessities of the Church and of Christendom. While the Irish-Scots occupied the islands and part of the western coast of Caledonia, all the north and east—that is to say, by far the greater part of the country—

was inhabited by the Picts, who were still heathens. Originally from Sarmatia, according to Tacitus—according to Bede, descendants of the Scythians—these primitive inhabitants of Great Britain, who had remained untouched by Roman or Christian influences, owed their name to their custom of fighting naked, and of painting their bodies in various colours, which had been the wont of all the ancient Britons at the time of Cæsar's invasion. The holy bishop Ninian more than a century before had preached the Christian faith to the Southern Picts —that is to say, to those who lived on the banks of the Forth or scattered among the Britons in the districts south of that river. But while even the traces of Ninian's apostolic work seemed at that moment effaced, although destined afterwards to reappear, the great majority of the Picts—those who inhabited the vast tracts to the north of the Grampians, into which no missionary before Columba had ever dared to penetrate—had always continued heathen. The thirty-four years of life which Columba had still before him were chiefly spent in missions, undertaken for the purpose of carrying the faith to the hilly straths, and into the deep glens and numerous islands of northern Caledonia. There dwelt a race, warlike, grasping, and bold, as inaccessible to softness as to fear, only half clothed notwithstanding the severity of the climate, and obstinately attached to their customs, belief, and chiefs. The missionary had to preach, to convert, and even at need to brave those formidable tribes, in whom Tacitus recognised the farthest off of the earth's inhabitants, and the last champions of freedom—"*terrarum ac libertatis extremos;*" those barbarians who, having gloriously resisted Agricola, drove the frightened Romans from Britain, and devastated and desolated the entire island up to the arrival of the Saxons; and whose descendants, after filling the history of Scotland with their feats of arms, have given, under the name of *Highlanders*, to the fallen Stuarts their most dauntless defenders, and to modern England her most glorious soldiers.

Columba crossed again and again that central mountain-range in which rise those waters which flow, some north and west to fall into the Atlantic Ocean, and some to the south to swell the North Sea—a range which the biographer of the saint calls the backbone of Britain (*dorsum Britanniæ*), and which separates the counties of Inverness and Argyll, as now existing, from the county of Perth, and includes the districts so well known to travellers under the names of Breadalbane, Atholl, and the Grampians. This was the recognised boundary between the Scots and Picts, and it was here that the ancestors of the latter, the heroic soldiers of Galgacus, had held their ground against the father-in-law of Tacitus, who even when victorious did not venture to cross that barrier. Often, too, Columba followed the course of that long valley of waters, which, to the north of these mountains, traverses

Scotland diagonally from the south-west, near Iona, to the north-east beyond Inverness. This valley is formed by a series of long gulfs and of inland lakes, which modern industry has linked together, making it possible for boats to pass from one sea to the other without making the long round by the Orcadian Isles. Thirteen centuries ago religion alone could undertake the conquest of those wild and picturesque regions, which a scanty but fierce and suspicious population disputed with the fir-forests and vast tracts of fern and heather, which are still to be encountered there.

The first glance thrown by history upon this watery highway discovers there the preaching and miracles of Columba. He was the first to traverse in his little skiff Loch Ness and the river which issues from it; he penetrated thus, after a long and painful journey, to the principal fortress of the Pictish king, the site of which is still shown upon a rock north of the town of Inverness. This powerful and redoubtable monarch, whose name was Bruidh or Brude, son of Malcolm, gave at first a very inhospitable reception to the Irish missionary. The companions of the saint relate that, priding himself upon the royal magnificence of his fortress, he gave orders that the gates should not be opened to the unwelcome visitor; but this was not a command to alarm Columba. He went up to the gateway, made the sign of the cross upon the two gates, and then knocked with his hand. Immediately the bars and bolts drew back, the gates rolled upon their hinges and were thrown wide open, and Columba entered like a conqueror. The king, though surrounded by his council, among whom no doubt were his heathen priests, was struck with panic; he hastened to meet the missionary, addressed to him pacific and encouraging words, and from that moment gave him every honour. It is not recorded whether Bruidh himself became a Christian, but during all the rest of his life he remained the friend and protector of Columba. He confirmed to him the possession of Iona, the sovereignty of which he seems to have disputed with his rival the king of the Dalriadian Scots, and our exile thus saw his establishment placed under the double protection of the two powers which shared Caledonia between them.

But the favour of the king did not bring with it that of the heathen priests, who are indicated by the Christian historians under the name of Druids or Magi, and who made an energetic and persevering resistance to the new apostle. These priests do not seem either to have taught or practised the worship of idols, but rather that of natural forces, and especially of the sun and other celestial bodies. They followed or met the Irish preacher in his apostolic journeys, less to refute his arguments than to hold back and intimidate those whom his preaching gained to Christ. The religious and supernatural character which was attributed by the Druids of Gaul to the woods and ancient trees, was attached by those of Caledonia to the streams and fountains, some of which were, according to their belief, salutary and beneficial, while others were deadly to man. Columba made special efforts to forbid among the new Christians the worship of sacred fountains, and, braving the threats of the Druids, drank in their presence the water which they affirmed would kill any man who dared to put it to his lips. But they used no actual violence against the stranger whom their prince had taken under his protection. One day, when Columba and his monks came out of the enclosure of the fort in which the king resided, to chant vespers according to the monastic custom, the Druids attempted to prevent them from singing, lest the sound of the religious chants should reach the people; but the abbot instantly intoned the sixty-fourth psalm, "*Eructavit cor meum verbum bonum: dico opera mea regi,*" with so formidable a voice, that he reduced his adversaries to silence, and made the surrounding spectators, and even the king himself, tremble before him.

But he did not confine himself to chanting in Latin; he preached. The dialect of the Picts, however, being different from that of the Scots, and unknown to him, it was necessary to employ the services of an interpreter. But his words were not the less efficacious on this account, though everywhere he was met by the rival exhortations or derisions of the pagan priests. His impassioned nature, as ready to love as to hate, made itself as apparent in his apostolic preachings as formerly in the struggles of his youth; and ties of tender intimacy, active and never appealed to in vain, were soon formed between himself and his converts. One of the Picts, who, having heard him preach by his interpreter, was converted with his wife and all his family, became his friend, and received many visits from him. One of the sons of this new convert fell dangerously ill; the Druids profited by the misfortune to reproach the anxious parents, making it appear that the sickness of their child was the punishment of their apostasy, and boasting the power of the ancient gods of the country, as superior to that of the Christian's God. Columba having been informed hastened to his friend's aid: when he arrived the child had just expired. As soon as he had done all that in him lay to console the father and mother, he asked to be allowed to enter alone into the place where the body of the child was. There he kneeled down and prayed long, bathed in tears; then rising, he said, "In the name of the Lord Jesus Christ, return to life and arise!" At the same moment the soul came back to the child's body. Columba helped him to rise, supported him, led him out of the cabin, and restored him to his parents. The power of prayer was thus as great, says Adamnan, in our saint as in Elijah and Elisha under the old law, or in St Peter, St Paul, and St John under the new.

While thus preaching faith and the grace of God by the voice of an interpreter, he at the same time recognised, admired, and proclaimed among those savage tribes the lights and virtues of the law of nature. He discovered the rays of its radiance in many an unknown hearer, by the help of that supernatural gift which enabled him to read the secrets of the heart, and to penetrate the darkness of the future; a gift which developed itself more and more in him as his apostolical career went on. One day while labouring in his evangelical work in the principal island of the Hebrides, the one which lies nearest to the mainland—Skye—he cried out all at once, " My sons, to-day you will see an ancient Pictish chief, who has kept faithfully all his life the precepts of the natural law, arrive in this island; he comes to be baptised and to die." Immediately after, a boat was seen to approach the shore with a feeble old man seated in the prow, who was recognised as the chief of one of the neighbouring tribes. Two of his companions took him up in their arms and brought him before the missionary, to whose words, as repeated by the interpreter, he listened attentively. When the discourse was ended the old man asked to be baptised; and immediately after breathed his last breath, and was buried in the very spot where he had just been brought to shore.

At a later date, in one of his last missions, when, himself an old man, he travelled along the banks of Loch Ness, always in the district to the north of the mountain-range of the *dorsum Britanniæ*, he said to the disciples who accompanied him, "Let us make haste and meet the angels who have come down from heaven, and who wait for us beside a Pict who has done well according to the natural law during his whole life to extreme old age: we must baptise him before he dies." Then hastening his steps and outstripping his disciples, as much as was possible at his great age, he reached a retired valley, now called Glen Urquhart, where he found the old man who awaited him. Here there was no longer any need of an interpreter, which makes it probable that Columba in his old age had learned the Pictish dialect. The old Pict heard him preach, was baptised, and with joyful serenity gave up to God the soul which was awaited by those angels whom Columba saw.

In this generous heart humanity claimed its rights no less than justice. It was in the name of humanity, his biographer expressly tells us, that he begged the freedom of a young female slave, born in Ireland, and the captive of one of the principal Druids or Magi. This Druid was named Broïchan, and lived with the king, whose foster-father he was, a tie of singular force and authority among the Celtic nations. Either from a savage pride, or out of enmity to the new religion, the Druid obstinately and cruelly refused the prayer of Columba. "Be it so," said the apostle; "but learn, Broïchan, that if thou refusest to set free this foreign captive, thou shalt die before I leave the province." When he had said this he left the castle, directing his steps towards that river Ness which appears so often in his history. But he was soon overtaken by two horsemen who came from the king to tell him that Broïchan, the victim of an accident, was dying, and fully disposed to set the young Irish girl free. The saint took up from the river bank a pebble, which he blessed, and gave to two of his monks, with the assurance that the sick man would be healed by drinking water in which this stone had been steeped, but only on the express condition that the captive should be delivered. She was immediately put under the charge of Columba's companions, and was thus restored at the same moment to her country and her freedom.

The Druid, though healed, was not thereby rendered less hostile to the apostle. Like the magicians of Pharaoh, he attempted to raise nature and her forces against the new Moses. On the day fixed for his departure, Columba found, on reaching, followed by a numerous crowd, the banks of the long and narrow lake from which the Ness issues, and by which he meant to travel, a strong contrary wind and thick fog, as Broïchan had threatened, which the Druids exulted to see. But Columba, entering his boat, bade the frightened rowers set the sail against the wind, and the assembled people saw him proceed rapidly on his course, as if borne by favourable breezes, towards the south end of the lake, by which he returned to Iona. But he left only to make a speedy return, and came so often as to accomplish the conversion of the Pictish nation, by destroying for ever the authority of the Druids in this last refuge of Celtic paganism. This sanguinary and untamable race was finally conquered by the Irish missionary. Before he ended his glorious career he had sown their forests, their defiles, their inaccessible mountains, their savage moors, and scarcely inhabited islands, with churches and monasteries.

Columba's assistants, in his numerous missions among the Picts, were the monks who had come with him, or who had followed him from Ireland. The fame of the obscure benefactors and civilisers of so distant a region has still more completely disappeared than that of Columba: it is with difficulty that some lingering trace of them is to be disentangled from the traditions of some churches whose sites may yet be found upon the ancient maps of Scotland. Such was Malruve (642-722), a kinsman of Columba, and like him descended from the royal race of Niall, but educated in the great Monastery of Bangor, which he left to follow his illustrious cousin into Albyn, passing by Iona. He must have long survived Columba, for he was for fifty-one years abbot of a community at Apercrossan—now Applecross—upon the north-west coast of Caledonia, opposite the large island of Skye, before he met his death, which was, according to local tradition, by the sword of Norwegian pirates.

Upon the opposite shore, in that striking promontory which forms the eastern extremity of Scotland, a district now known as Buchan, various churches trace their origin to Columba, and to one of his Irish disciples called Drostan. The *mor-maer* or chief of the country had at first refused them his permission to settle there, but his son fell dangerously ill, and he hastened after the missionaries, offering them the land necessary for their foundation, and begging them to pray for the dying boy. They prayed, and the child was saved. After having blessed the new church, and predicted that none who profaned it should ever conquer their enemies or enjoy long life, Columba installed his companions in their new home, and himself turned to continue his journey. When Drostan saw himself thus condemned to live at a distance from his master, he could not restrain his tears; for these old saints, in their wild and laborious career, loved each other with a passionate tenderness, which is certainly not the least touching feature in their character, and which places an inextinguishable light upon their heads amid the darkness of the legends. "Then," Columba said, "let us call this place the Monastery of Tears;" and the great abbey — that of Deir — which lasted a thousand years upon that spot, always retained the name. "He who sows in tears shall reap in joy."

CHAPTER IV.

Columba consecrates the King of the Scots. — He goes to the National Assembly of Ireland, defends the Independence of the Hiberno-Scotic Colony, and saves the Corporation of Bards.

T would not, however, be natural to suppose that the mission of Columba among the Picts could entirely absorb his life and soul. That faithful love for his race and country which had moved him with compassion for the young Irish girl in captivity among the Picts did not permit him to remain indifferent to the wars and revolutions which were at the bottom of all national life among the Irish Scots as well as the Irish colony in Scotland. There was not a more marked feature in his character than his constant solicitude, his compassionate sympathy, as well after as before his removal to Iona, for the bloody struggles in which his companions and relatives in Ireland were so

often engaged. Nothing was nearer to his heart than the claim of kindred; for that reason alone he occupied himself without ceasing with the affairs of individual relatives. "This man," he said to himself, "is of my race; I must help him. It is my duty to pray for him, because he is of the same stock as myself. This other is of kin to my mother," &c. And then he would add, "My friends and kindred, who are descended like me from the Nialls, see how they fight!" And from the far distance of his desert isle he fought with them in heart and thought, as of old he had aided them in person. He breathed from afar the air of battle; he divined the issue by what his companions considered a prophetic instinct, and told it to his monks, to his Irish countrymen, and to the Caledonian Scots who sought him in his new dwelling. With better reason still his soul kindled within him when he foresaw any struggle in which his new neighbours the Dalriadian colonists were to be engaged, either with the Picts, whom they were one day to conquer, or with the Anglo-Saxons.

One day towards the end of his life, being alone with Diarmid his minister (as the monk attached to his personal service was called), he cried out all at once, "The bell! let the bell be rung instantly!" The bell of the modest monastery was nothing better than one of the little square bells made of beaten iron, which are still shown in Irish museums, exactly similar to those which are worn by the cattle in Spain and the Jura. It was enough for the necessities of the little insular community. At its sound the monks hastened to throw themselves on their knees around their father. "Now," said he, "let us pray—let us pray with intense fervour for our people, and for King Aïdan; for at this very moment the battle has begun between them and the barbarians." When their prayers had lasted some time, he said, "Behold, the barbarians flee! Aïdan is victorious!"

The barbarians, against whom Columba rang his bells and called for the prayers of his monks, were the Anglo-Saxons of Northumbria, who were still pagans, and whose descendants were destined to owe the inestimable blessings of Christianity to the monks of Iona and the spiritual posterity of Columba. But at that time the invaders thought only of taking a terrible revenge for the evils which Britain, before they conquered it, had endured from Scoto-Pictish incursions, and of extending their power ever farther and farther on the Caledonian side. As for King Aïdan, he had replaced his cousin-german, King Connall, who had guaranteed to Columba the possession of Iona, as chief of the Dalriadian colony in Argyll. His accession to the throne took place in 574, eleven years after the arrival of Columba; and nothing proves more fully the influence acquired by the Irish missionary during this short interval than Aïdan's resolution to have his coronation blessed by the Abbot of Iona.

Columba, though his friend, did not wish him to be king, preferring his brother; but an angel appeared to him three times in succession, and commanded him to consecrate Aïdan according to the ceremony prescribed in a book covered with crystal which was left with him for that purpose. Columba, who was then in a neighbouring island, went back to Iona, where he was met by the new king. The abbot, obedient to the celestial vision, laid his hands upon the head of Aïdan, blessed him, and ordained him king. He inaugurated thus not only a new kingdom, but a new rite, which became at a later date the most august solemnity of Christian national life. The coronation of Aïdan is the first authentic instance known in the West. Columba thus assumed, in respect to the Scotic or Dalriadian kingdom, the same authority with which the abbots of Armagh, successors of St Patrick, were already invested in respect to the kings of Ireland. That this supreme authority and these august functions were conferred upon abbots instead of bishops, has been the cause of much surprise. But at that period of the ecclesiastical history of Celtic nations the episcopate was entirely in the shade; the abbots and monks alone appear to have been great and influential, and the successors of St Columba long retained this singular supremacy over the bishops.

According to Scotch national tradition, the new king Aïdan was consecrated by Columba upon a great stone called the Stone of Destiny. This stone was afterwards transferred to Dunstaffnage Castle, the ruins of which may be seen upon the coast of Argyll, not far from Iona; then to the Abbey of Scone, near Perth; and was finally carried away by Edward I., the cruel conqueror of Scotland, to Westminster, where it still serves as a pedestal for the throne of the kings of England on the day of their coronation. The solemn inauguration of the kingdom of Aïdan marks the historical beginning of the Scotch monarchy, which before that period was more or less fabulous. Aïdan was the first prince of the Scots who passed from the rank of territorial chief to that of independent king, and head of a dynasty whose descendants were one day to reign over the three kingdoms of Great Britain.

But to secure the independence of the new Scottish royalty, or rather of the young nation whose stormy and poetic history was thus budding under the breath and blessing of Columba, it was necessary to break the link of subjugation or vassalage which bound the Dalriadian colony to the Irish kings. All this time it had remained tributary to the monarchs of the island which it had left nearly a century before to establish itself in Caledonia. To obtain by peaceable means the abolition of this tribute, Columba—who was Irish by heart as well as by birth, yet who at the same time was, like the Dalriadians, his kinsmen, an emigrant in Caledonia, and, like the new king, descended from the monarchs of Ireland—must have seemed the mediator indicated by nature. He accepted the mission, and returned to Ireland, which he had thought never to see again, in company with the king whom he had just crowned, to endeavour to come to an agreement with the Irish monarch and the other princes and chiefs assembled at Drumkeath. His impartiality was above all suspicion; for the very day of the coronation of Aïdan he had announced to him, in the name of God, that the prosperity of the new Scotic kingdom depended upon peace with Ireland, its cradle. In the midst of the ceremony he had said aloud to the king whom he had crowned, "Charge your sons, and let them charge their grandchildren, never to expose their kingdom to be lost by their fault. The moment that they attempt any fraudulent enterprise against my spiritual descendants here, or against my countrymen and kindred in Ireland, the hand of God will weigh heavily upon them, the heart of men will be raised against them, and the victory of their enemies will be assured."

The king of Ireland, Diarmid, who was, like Columba, of the race of Niall, but of the Nialls of the North, and whom our saint had so violently resisted, had died immediately after the voluntary exile of Columba. He perished, as has been mentioned, by the hand of a prince called Black Aedh, chief of the Antrim Dalriadians, who remained in Ireland when a part of their clan emigrated to Scotland. Some time afterwards the supreme throne of Ireland fell to another Aedh, of the southern branch of the race of Niall, and consequently of the same stock as Columba. He was also the friend and benefactor of his emigrant cousin, to whom he had given before his exile the site of Derry, the most important of his Irish foundations. The first synod or parliament of Aedh's reign had been convoked in a place called Drumceitt, now Drumkeath, the *Whale's Back*, situated in his special patrimony, not far from the sea and the gulf of Lough Foyle, where Columba had embarked, and at the further end of which was his dear monastery of Derry. It was there that he returned with his royal client, the new king of the Caledonian Scots, whose confessor, or, as the Irish termed it, *friend of his soul*, he had become. The two kings, Aedh and Aïdan, presided at this assembly, which sat for fourteen months, and the recollection of which has been preserved among the Irish people, the most faithful nation in the world, for more than a thousand years.

The Irish lords and clergy encamped under tents like soldiers during the entire duration of this parliament. The most important question discussed among them was no doubt that of the tribute exacted from the king of the Dalriadians. It does not appear that the Irish king demanded tribute on account of the new kingdom founded by his ancient subjects, but rather on account of that part of Ireland itself, at present the county of Antrim, from whence the Dalriadian colonists had gone, and which was the hereditary patrimony of their new king. This was precisely the position in which the Norman princes, who had become kings of England, while still dukes of Normandy, found themselves, five centuries later, in respect to the kings of France. Columba, the friend of both kings, was commissioned to solve the difficulty. According to some Irish authors, the Abbot of Iona, when the decisive moment arrived, refused to decide, and transferred to another monk, St Colman, the responsibility of pronouncing the judgment. At all events, the Irish king renounced all suzerainty over the king of the Dalriadians of *Albania*, as Scotland was then called. Independence and freedom from all tribute were granted to the Albanian Scots, who, on their side, promised perpetual alliance and hospitality to their Irish countrymen.

Columba had another cause to plead at the parliament of Drumceitt, which was almost as dear to his heart as the independence of the Scotic kingdom and colony of which he was the spiritual head. The question in this case was nothing less than that of the existence of a corporation as powerful as, and more ancient and national than, the clergy itself: it concerned the bards, who were at once poets and genealogists, historians and musicians, and whose high position and popular ascendancy form one of the most characteristic features of Irish history. The entire nation, always enamoured of its traditions, its fabulous antiquity, and local and domestic glory, surrounded with ardent and respectful sympathy the men who could clothe in a poetic dress all the lore and superstitions of the past, as well as the passions and interests of the present. In the annals of Ireland, as far back as they can be traced, the bards or *ollambh*, who were regarded as oracles of knowledge, of poetry, history, and music, are always to be found. They were trained from their infancy with the greatest care in special communities, and so greatly honoured that the first place at the royal table, after that of the king himself, was reserved for them. Since the introduction of Christianity, the bards, like the Druids of earlier times, whose successors they are supposed to have been, continued to form a powerful and popular band. They were then divided into three orders : the *Fileas*, who sang of religion and of war ; the *Brehons*, whose name is associated with the ancient laws of the country, which they versified and recited ; the *Seanachies*, who enshrined in verse the national history and antiquities, and, above all, the genealogies and prerogatives of the ancient families who were specially dear to the national and warlike passions of the Irish people. They carried this guardianship of historical recollections and relics so far as to watch over the boundaries of each province and family domain. They took part, like the clergy, in all the assemblies, and with still greater reason in all the fights. They were overwhelmed with favours and privileges by the kings and petty princes, on whom their songs and their harp could alone bestow a place in history, or even a good name among their contemporaries. But naturally this great power had produced many abuses, and at the moment of which we speak, the popularity of the bards had suffered an eclipse. A violent opposition had been raised against them. Their great number, their insolence, their insatiable greed, had all been made subjects of reproach ; and, above all, they were censured for having made traffic and a trade of their poetry—of lavishing praises upon the nobles and princes who were liberal to them, and making others the subject of satirical invectives, which the charm of their verse spread but too readily, to the great injury of the honour of families. The enmities raised against them had come to such a point, that King Aedh felt himself in sufficient force to propose to the assembly of Drumceitt the radical abolition of this dangerous order, and the banishment, and even outlawry, if not, as some say, the massacre, of all the bards.

It is not apparent that the clergy took any part whatever in this persecution of a body which they might well have regarded as their rivals. The introduction of Christianity into the country of Ossian, under St Patrick, seems scarcely, if at all, to have affected the position of the bards. They became Christians without either inflicting or suffering any violence, and they were in general the auxiliaries and friends of the bishops, monks, and saints. Each monastery, like each prince and lord, possessed a bard, whose office it was to sing the glory, and often to write the annals, of the community. Notwithstanding, it is apparent through many of the legends of the period, that the bards represented a pagan power, in the eyes of many ecclesiastical writers, and that they were willingly identified with those Druids or Magi who had been the principal enemies of the evangelical mission of Patrick in Ireland and of Columba in Scotland. Even in the legend of Columba it is noted that some among them had determined to make him pay for his ransom according to their custom, and had for this end addressed to him importunate solicitations, threatening, if he refused, to abuse him in their verse.

Notwithstanding, it was Columba who saved them. He who was born a poet and remained a poet to the last day of his life, interceded for them, and gained their cause. His success was not without difficulty, for King Aedh was eager in their pursuit; but Columba, as stubborn as bold, made head against all. He represented that care must be taken not to pull up the good corn with the tares; that the general exile of the poets would be the death of a venerable antiquity and of that poetry which was so dear to the country and so useful to those who knew how to employ it. The ripe corn must not be burned, he said, because of the weeds that mingle with it. The king and the assembly yielded at length, under condition that the number of bards should be henceforward limited, and that their profession should be put under certain rules determined by Columba himself. It was his eloquence alone which turned aside the blow by which they were threatened; and knowing themselves to be saved by him, they showed their gratitude by exalting his glory in their songs and by leaving to their successors the charge of continuing his praise.

Columba himself had a profound pleasure in this poetical popularity. The corporation of bards had a chief, Dallan Fergall, who was blind, and whose violent death (he was murdered by pirates) has given him a place among the holy martyrs, of whom there are so few in Ireland. Immediately after the favourable decision of the assembly, Dallan composed a song in honour of Columba, and came to sing it before him. At the flattering sounds of this song of gratitude the Abbot of Iona could not defend himself from a human sentiment of self-satisfaction. But he was immediately reproved by one of his monks, Baithen, one of his twelve original companions in exile, and who was destined to be his successor. This faithful friend was not afraid to accuse Columba of pride, nor to tell him that he saw a sombre cloud of demons flying and playing round his head. Columba profited by the warning. He imposed silence upon Dallan, reminding him that it was only the dead who should be praised, and absolutely forbade him to repeat his song. Dallan obeyed reluctantly, and awaited the death of the saint to make known his poem, which became celebrated in Irish literature under the name of *Ambhra*, or the *Praise of St Columbcille*. It was still sung a century after his death throughout all Ireland and Scotland, and even the least devout of men repeated it with tenderness and fervour, as a safeguard against the dangers of war and every other accident. It even came to be believed that every one who knew this Ambhra by heart and sang it piously would die a good death. But when the unenlightened people came so far as to believe that even great sinners, without either conversion or penitence, had only to sing the Ambhra of Columbcille every day in order to be saved, a wonder happened, says the historian and grandnephew of the saint, which opened the eyes of the faithful, by showing to them how they ought to understand the privileges accorded by God to His saints. An ecclesiastic of the metropolitan church of Armagh, who was a man of corrupt life, and desired to be saved without making any change in his conduct, succeeded in learning the half of the famous Ambhra, but never could remember the other half. It was in vain that he made a pilgrimage to the tomb of the saint, fasted, prayed, and spent the entire night in efforts to impress it upon his memory — the next morning he found that, though he had at length succeeded in learning the latter half, he had completely forgotten the first.

The gratitude of the bards to him who had preserved them from exile and outlawry has certainly had some share in the wonderful and lasting popularity of Columba's name. Shrined in the national and religious poetry of the two islands, his fame has not only lasted in full brilliancy in Ireland, but it has survived even the Reformation—which has destroyed almost all other traces of their past history as Christians—in the memory of the Celts of Scotland.

On the other hand, the protection of Columba certainly confirmed the popularity of the bards in the heart of the Irish nation. All opposition between the religious spirit and the bardic influence disappeared from his time. Music and poetry after that period identified themselves more and more with ecclesiastical life. Among the relics of the saints the harps on which they had played found a place. At the first English conquest the bishops and abbots excited the surprise of the invaders by their love of music, and by accompanying themselves on the harp. Irish poetry, which was in the days of Patrick and Columba so powerful and so popular, has long undergone in the country of Ossian the same fate as the religion of which these great saints were the apostles. Rooted like it in the heart of a conquered people, and like it proscribed and persecuted with unwearying vehemence, it has come ever forth anew from the bloody furrow in which it was supposed to be buried. The bards became the most powerful allies of patriotism, the most dauntless prophets of national independence, and also the favourite victims of the cruelty of spoilers and conquerors. They made music and poetry weapons and bulwarks against foreign oppression, and the oppressors used them as they had used the priests and the nobles. A price was set upon their heads. But while the last scions of the royal and noble races, decimated or ruined in Ireland, departed, to die out under a foreign sky amid the miseries of exile, the successor of the bards, the minstrel, whom nothing could tear from his native soil, was pursued, tracked, and taken like a wild beast, or chained and slaughtered like the most dangerous of rebels.

In the annals of the atrocious legislation directed by the English against the Irish people, as well before as after the Reformation, special penalties against the *minstrels, bards, rhymers,* and *genealogists,* who sustained the lords and gentlemen in their love of rebellion and of other crimes, are to be met at every step. An attempt was made, under the sanguinary Elizabeth, to give pecuniary recompense to those who would celebrate "her Majesty's most worthy praise." The bargain was accepted by none. All preferred flight or death to this salary of lies. Wandering over hill and dale, hidden in the depths of the devastated country, they perpetuated there the poetic traditions of their condemned race, and sang the glory of ancient heroes and new martyrs, the shame of apostates, and the crimes of the sacrilegious stranger.

In order the better to brave tyranny in the midst of a subdued and silent people, they had recourse to allegory and the elegies of love. Under the figure of an enslaved queen—or of a woman loved with an everlasting love and fought for with despairing faithfulness, in face of the jealous fury of a stepmother—they celebrated again and again the Irish Fatherland, the country in mourning and tears, once queen and now a slave. The Irish, says a great historian of our own day, loved to make of their country a real being whom they loved, and who loved them. They loved to address her without naming her name, and to identify the austere and perilous devotion which they had vowed to her with all that is sweetest and most fortunate in the affections of the heart, like those Spartans who crowned themselves with flowers when about to perish at Thermopylæ.

Up to the time of the ungrateful Stuarts, this proscription of the national poets was permanent, increasing in force with every change of reign and every new parliament. The rage of the Cromwellian Protestants carried them so far as to break, wherever they met with them, the minstrel's harps which were still to be found in the miserable cottages of the starving Irish, as they were eleven centuries before, at the time when the courageous and charitable Bridget saw them suspended on the wall of the king's palace. Nevertheless the harp has remained the emblem of Ireland even in the official arms of the British Empire; and during all last century the travelling harper, last and pitiful successor of the bards protected by Columba, was always to be found at the side of the priest to celebrate the holy mysteries of the proscribed worship. He never ceased to be received with tender respect under the thatched roof of the poor Irish peasant, whom he consoled in his misery and oppression by the plaintive tenderness and solemn sweetness of the music of his fathers.

The continuance of these distinctive features of Irish character through so many centuries is so striking, and the misfortunes of that noble race touch us so nearly, that it is difficult to resist the temptation of leaving behind us those distant ages, and of following through later generations the melancholy relics of all that has been discovered or admired in the most ancient days. We may be pardoned for adding that, if the text of those poetic and generously obstinate protests against the enslavement of Ireland have perished, the life and spirit of them has survived in the pure and penetrating beauty of the ancient Irish airs. Their harmonies and their refrains, which are inimitably natural, original, and pathetic, move the depths of the soul, and send a thrill through all the fibres of human sensibility. Thomas Moore, in adapting to them words which are marked with the impression of a passionate fidelity to the proscribed faith and oppressed country, has given to the 'Irish Melodies' a popularity which was not the least powerful among those pleas which determined the great contest of Catholic Emancipation.

The genius of Celtic poetry has, however, survived not only in Ireland, in the country of Columba and of Moore, but has found a refuge in the glens of the Scottish Highlands, among those vast moors and rugged mountains, and beside the deep and narrow lakes, which Columba, bearing the light of the faith to the Caledonian Picts, had so often traversed. In those districts where, as in a great part of Ireland, the Erse or Gaelic language is still spoken, the Celtic muse, always sad and always attached to the cause of the people, has been found in recent times, at the most prosaic moment of modern civilisation, in the eighteenth century itself, inspiring the warlike songs and laments which the Highlanders have consecrated to the conquered Pretender and his followers slain. And if we may believe a competent and impartial judge—Charles Mackay, in his Introduction to the 'Jacobite Songs and Ballads of Scotland'—the last effusions of the soul of the Gaelic race surpass, in plaintive beauty and in passionate feeling, even those delicious Anglo-Scottish songs which no traveller can hear without emotion, and which have assured the palm, at least of poetry, to the cause of the Stuarts, which has been so sadly represented by its princes, and so ill served by events, but which the popular and national muse has thus avenged, even for the irremediable defeat of Culloden.

CHAPTER V.

Columba's Relations with Ireland—Continued.

N the national parliament of Drumceitt which saved the bards, and where all the ecclesiastical chiefs of the Irish nation, along with their princes and provincial kings, were assembled, Columba, already invested by his apostolical labours with great power and authority, found himself surrounded by public homage, and tokens of universal confidence. To all the kings, whose kinsman and friend he was, he preached peace, concord, the pardon of affronts, and the recall of exiles, many of whom had found shelter in the island monastery which owed its existence to his own exile. Nevertheless, it was not without trouble that he obtained from the supreme monarch the freedom of a young prince, named Scandlan, son of the chief of Ossory, whom Aedh detained in prison, in contempt of his sworn faith, and of an agreement to which Columba himself

had been a witness. The noble abbot went to the prisoner in his dungeon, blessed him, and predicted to him that he should be twice exiled, but that he should survive his oppressor, and reign for thirty years in his paternal domain. The king yielded on this point, but with a bad grace; he feared the influence of the illustrious exile, and had seen him return to Ireland with dissatisfaction. His eldest son had publicly ridiculed the monks of Iona, and had thus drawn upon himself the curse of Columba, which brought misfortune, for he was afterwards dethroned and assassinated. But the king's second son Domnall, who was still young, took openly the part of the Abbot of Iona, who predicted for him not only a long and glorious reign, but the rare privilege of dying in his bed, on the condition of receiving the Holy Communion every eight days, and of keeping at least one in seven of his promises —a somewhat satirical limit, which betrays either the old contradictory spirit of the converted Niall, or the recollection of his own legitimate resentment against certain princes. His prophecy, extremely improbable as it was, in a country where all the princes perished on the battle-field or by a violent death, was nevertheless fulfilled. Domnall, who was the third successor of his father, following after two other kings who were destroyed by their enemies, had a long and prosperous reign; he gained numerous victories, marching to battle under a banner blessed by St Columba, and died, after an illness of eighteen months, in his bed, or, as Columba specified, with a precision which marks the rareness of the occurrence, on his down-bed. His father, although reconciled to Columba, did not escape the common law. The great abbot bestowed upon him his monastic cowl, promising that it should always be to him as an impenetrable cuirass. After this, he never went into battle without putting on his friend's cowl above his armour. But one day when he had forgotten it, he was killed in a combat with the king of Lagenia or Leinster. Columba had previously warned him against waging war with the people of Leinster, which was the country of his mother, and which he loved with that impassioned clan or family affection which is so distinctive a feature in his character. The Lagenians had not lost the opportunity of working upon this sentiment: for one day, when he was at his Abbey of Durrow, upon their boundary, a numerous assembly of all ages, from children to old men, came to him, and, surrounding him, pleaded with such animation their kindred with his mother, that they obtained from him the promise, or prophecy, that no king should ever be able to overcome them, so long as they fought for a just cause.

There is no doubt that, after the assembly of Drumceitt, Columba made many journeys to Ireland. The direction of the various monasteries which he had founded there before his voluntary exile, and of which he had kept the government in his own hands, must have led him often back; but after that assembly, his visits were always made notable by miracles of healing, prophecy, or revelation, and still more by the tender solicitude of his paternal heart. Sometimes, towards the decline of his life, while traversing a hilly or marshy country, he travelled in a car, as St Patrick had done; but the care with which his biographers note this fact, proves that formerly the greater part of his journeys had been made on foot. He did not limit himself to communities of which he was the superior or founder; he loved to visit other monastic sanctuaries also, such as that of Clanmacnoise, the importance of which has already been pointed out. And on such occasions the crowding and eagerness of the monks to pay their homage to the holy and beloved old man was redoubled; they left their outdoor work, and, crossing the earthen intrenchment, which, like the *vallum* of Roman camps, enclosed the Celtic monasteries, came to meet him, chanting hymns. When they came up to him, they prostrated themselves on the ground at his feet, ere they embraced him; and in order to shelter him from the crowd during the solemn processions which were made in his honour, a rampart of branches was carried like a dais by four men, who surrounded him, treading with equal steps. An ancient author even goes so far as to say, that on the occasion of his return and prolonged stay in his native country, he was invested with a sort of general supremacy over all the religious of Ireland, both monks and nuns.

During the journey from Durrow to Clonmacnoise, Columba made a halt at one of his own monasteries, where a poor little scholar, "of thick speech, and still more heavy aspect," whom his superiors employed in the meanest services, glided into the crowd, and, stealthily approaching the great abbot, touched the end of his robe behind him, as the Canaanitish woman touched the robe of our Lord. Columba, perceiving it, stopped, turned round, and, taking the child by the neck, kissed him. "Away, away, little fool!" cried all the spectators. "Patience, my brethren," said Columba: then turning to the boy, who trembled with fear, "My son," he said, "open thy mouth, and show me thy tongue." The child obeyed, with increasing timidity. The abbot made the sign of the cross upon his tongue, and added, "This child, who appears to you so contemptible, let no one henceforward despise him. He shall grow every day in wisdom and virtue; he shall be reckoned with the greatest among you; God will give to this tongue, which I have just blessed, the gift of eloquence and true doctrine." The boy grew to manhood, and became celebrated in the churches of Scotland and Ireland, where he was venerated under the name of St Ernan. He himself told this prophecy, so well justified by the event, to a contemporary of Adamnan, who has preserved all the details for us.

These journeys, however, were not necessary to prove Columba's solicitude for the monks who filled his monasteries. He showed the same care when distant as when at hand, by the help of that miraculous foresight which came to the assistance of his paternal anxiety in all their spiritual and temporal necessities. One day, after his return from Ireland, he was heard to stop suddenly short in the correspondence or transcription in which he had been engaged in his little cell in Iona, and cry with all his strength, "Help, help!" This cry was addressed to the guardian angel of the community, and the appeal was made on behalf of a man who had fallen from the top of the round tower which was then being built at Durrow, in the centre of Ireland—so great was his confidence in what he himself called the indescribable and lightning speed of the flight of angels; and greater still was his trust in their protection. Another time, at Iona, in a day of chilly fog, such as occurs often in that sombre climate, he was suddenly seen to burst into tears. When asked the reason of his distress, he answered, "Dear son, it is not without reason that I weep. At this very hour I see my dear monks of Durrow condemned by their abbot to exhaust themselves in this dreary weather building the great round tower of the monastery, and the sight overwhelms me." The same day, and at the same hour, as was afterwards ascertained, Laisran, the abbot of Durrow, felt within himself something like an internal flame, which reawakened in his heart a sentiment of pity for his monks. He immediately commanded them to leave their work, to warm themselves, and take some food, and even forbade them to resume their building until the weather had improved. This same Laisran afterwards came to deserve the name of Consoler of the Monks, so much had he been imbued by Columba with that supernatural charity which, in monastic life, as in every other Christian existence, is at once a light and a flame, *ardens et lucens*.

Columba not only retained his superior jurisdiction over the monasteries which he had founded in Ireland, or which had been admitted to the privileges of his foundations, but he also exercised a spiritual authority, which it is difficult to explain, over various laymen of his native island. On one occasion, he is known to have sent his cousin, friend, and principal disciple to the centre of Ireland, to Drum-Cuill, to pronounce sentence of excommunication against a certain family, whose crime, however, is not specified. This disciple was Baithen, whom we have seen to be one of Columba's companions from the moment of his exile, and who warned his superior against the fumes of pride, at the time when the bards began to express their enthusiastic gratitude. The gentle Baithen, when he had arrived at the appointed place, after having passed the whole night in prayer under an oak, said to his companions, "No, I will not excommunicate this family before making sure that it will not repent. I give it a year's respite, and during the year, the fate of this tree shall be a warning to it." Some time after the tree was struck by lightning; but we are not informed if the family thus warned was brought to repentance.

Baithen was a man of tender soul, of whom we would fain speak at greater length, if it were not needful to circumscribe the wide and confused records of Celtic hagiography. Columba compared him to St John the Evangelist; he said that his beloved disciple resembled him who was the beloved disciple of Christ, by his exquisite purity, his penetrating simplicity, and his love of perfection. And Columba was not alone in doing justice to the man who, after having been his chief lieutenant in his work, was to become his first successor. One day, in an assembly of learned monks, probably held in Ireland, Fintan, a very learned and very wise man, and also one of the twelve companions of Columba's exile, was questioned upon the qualities of Baithen. "Know," he answered, "that there is no one on this side of the Alps who is equal to him in knowledge of the Scriptures, and in the greatness of his learning." "What!" said his questioners—"not even his master, Columba?" "I do not compare the disciple with the master," answered Fintan. "Columba is not to be compared with philosophers and learned men, but with patriarchs, prophets, and apostles. The Holy Ghost reigns in him; he has been chosen by God for the good of all. He is a sage among all sages, a king among kings, an anchorite with anchorites, a monk of monks; and in order to bring himself to the level even of laymen, he knows how to be poor of heart among the poor; thanks to the apostolic charity which inspires him, he can rejoice with the joyful, and weep with the unfortunate. And amid all the gifts which God's generosity has lavished on him, the true humility of Christ is so royally rooted in his soul, that it seems to have been born with him." It is added that all the learned hearers assented unanimously to this enthusiastic eulogium.

CHAPTER VI.

Columba the Protector of Sailors and Agriculturists, the Friend of Laymen, and the Avenger of the Oppressed.

DURING all the rest of his life, which was to pass in his island of Iona, or in the neighbouring districts of Scotland which had been evangelised by his unwearied zeal, nothing strikes and attracts the historian so much as the generous ardour of Columba's charity. The history of his whole life proves that he was born with a violent and even vindictive temper; but he had succeeded in subduing and transforming himself to such a point that he was ready to sacrifice all things to the love of his neighbour. It is not merely an apostle or a monastic founder whom we have before us—beyond and besides this it is a friend, a brother, a benefactor of men, a brave and untiring defender of the labourer, the feeble, and the poor: it is a man occupied not only with the salvation but also with the happiness, the rights, and the interests of all his fellow-creatures, and in whom the instinct of pity showed itself in a bold and continual interposition against all oppression and wickedness.

Without losing the imposing and solemn character which always accompanied his popular fame, he will now be revealed to us under a still more touching aspect, through all the long succession of his apostolic labours, and in the two principal occupations — agriculture and navigation — which gave variety to his missionary life.

For navigation alternated with agriculture in the labours of the cenobites of Iona. The same monks who cultivated the scanty fields of the holy island, and who reaped and thrashed the corn, accompanied Columba in his voyages to the neighbouring isles, and followed the sailor's trade, then, it would seem, more general than now among the Irish race. Communication was then frequent, not only between Ireland and Great Britain, but between Ireland and Gaul. We have already seen in the port of Nantes an Irish boat ready to carry away the founder of Luxeuil. The Gaulish merchants came to sell or offer their wines as far as to the centre of the island, to the Abbey of Clonmacnoise. In the life of our saint, seafaring populations are constantly spoken of as surrounding him, and receiving his continual visits; and exercises and excursions are also mentioned, which associate his disciples with all the incidents of a seafaring life. As a proof of this we quote four lines, in very ancient Irish, which may be thus translated:—

> "Honour to the soldiers who live at Iona;
> There are three times fifty under the monastic rule,
> Seventy of whom are appointed to row,
> And cross the sea in their leathern barks."

These boats were sometimes hollowed out of the trunks of trees, like those which are still found buried in the *bogs* or turf-mosses of Ireland; but most generally they were made of osier, and covered with buffalo-skins, like those described by Cæsar. Their size was estimated by the number of skins which had been used to cover them. They were generally small, and those made of one or two skins were portable. The abbot of Iona had one of this description for the inland waters when he travelled beyond the northern hills (*dorsum Britanniæ*), which he crossed so often to preach among the Picts. At a later period the community possessed many of a much larger size, to convey the materials for the reconstruction of the primitive monastery at Iona, and the timber which the sons of Columba cut down and fashioned in the vast oak forests which then covered the whole country, now so sadly deprived of wood. They went like galleys, with sail or oar, and were furnished with masts and rigging like modern boats. The holy island had at last an entire fleet at its disposal, manned and navigated by the monks.

In these frail skiffs Columba and his monks ploughed the dangerous and stormy sea which dashes on the coasts of Scotland and Ireland, and penetrated boldly into the numberless gulfs and straits of the sombre Hebridean archipelago. They knew the perils to which their insular existence exposed them; but they braved those dangers without fear, accustomed as they were to live in the midst of storms, upon an isle which the great waves of ocean threatened continually to swallow up. Not less alarming was their position when the winds carried them towards the terrible whirlpool, named, after a prince of the Niall family who had been drowned there, the Caldron of Brechan, and which there was always a risk of being driven upon while crossing from Ireland to Scotland. The winds, when blowing from certain directions, hollow out in their whirl such terrible abysses about this spot, that even to our own time it has continued the terror of sailors. The holiest of Columba's guests passed it by with trembling, raising their hands towards heaven to implore the miracle which alone could save them. But he himself, who one day was almost swallowed up in it, and whose mind was continually preoccupied by the recollection of his kindred, imagined that he saw in this whirlpool a symbol of the torments endured in purgatory by the soul of his relative who had perished at that spot, and of the duty of praying for the repose of that soul at the same time as he prayed for the safety of the companions of his voyage.

Columba's prayers, his special and ardently desired blessing, and his constant and passionate intercession for his brethren and disciples, were the grand safeguard of the navigators of Iona, not only against wind and shipwrecks, but against other dangers which have now disappeared from these coasts. Great fishes of the cetaceous order swarmed at that time in the Hebridean sea. The sharks ascended even into the Highland rivers, and one of the companions of Columba, swimming across the Ness, was saved only by the prayer of the saint, at the moment when he was but an oar's-length from the odious monster, which had before swallowed one of the natives. The entire crew of a boat manned by monks took fright and turned back one day on meeting a whale, or perhaps only a shark more formidable than its neighbours; but on another occasion, the same Baithen who was the friend and successor of Columba, encouraged by the holy abbot's blessing, had more courage, continued his course, and saw the monster bury itself in the waves. "After all," said the monk, "we are both in the hands of God, both this monster and I." Other monks, sailing in the high northern sea, were panic-struck by the appearance of hosts of unknown shellfish, which, attaching themselves to the oars and sides of the boat, made holes in the hide with which the framework was covered.

It was neither curiosity nor love of gain, nor even a desire to convert the pagans, which stimulated Columba's disciples to dare all the dangers of navigation in one of the most perilous seas of the world; it was the longing for solitude, the irresistible wish to find a more distant retreat, an asylum still further off than that of Iona, upon some unknown rock amid the loneliness of the sea, where no one could join them, and from which they never could be brought back. They returned to Iona without having discovered what they were in search of, sad yet not discouraged; and after an interval of rest always took to sea again, to begin once more their anxious search. It was thus that the steep and almost inaccessible island of St Kilda, made famous by the daring of its bird-hunters, was first discovered; then far to the north of the Hebrides, and even of the Orcades, they reached the Shetland Isles, and even, according to some, Iceland itself, which is only at the distance of a six days' voyage from Ireland, and where the first Christian church bore the name of St Columba. Another of their discoveries was the Faröe Islands, where the Norwegians at a later date found traces of the sojourn of the Irish monks, Celtic books, crosses, and bells. Cormac, the boldest of these bold explorers, made three long, laborious, and dangerous voyages with the hope, always disappointed, of finding the wilderness of which he dreamed. The first time on landing at Orkney he escaped death, with which the savage inhabitants of that archipelago threatened all strangers, only by means of the *recommendations* which Columba had procured from the Pictish king, himself converted, to the still pagan king of the northern islanders. On another occasion the south wind drove him for fourteen successive days and nights almost into the depths of the icy ocean, far beyond anything that the imagination of man had dreamed of in those days.

Columba, the father and head of those bold and pious mariners, followed and guided them by his ever vigilant and prevailing prayers. He was in some respects present with them, notwithstanding the distance which separated them from the sanctuary and from the island harbours which they had left. Prayer gave him an intuitive knowledge of the dangers they ran. He saw them, he suffered and trembled for them; and immediately assembling the brethren who remained in the monastery by the sound of the bell, offered for them the prayers of the community. He implored the Lord with tears to grant the change of wind which was necessary for those at sea, and did not rise from his knees until he had a certainty that his prayers were granted. This happened often, and the saved monks, on returning from their dangerous voyages, hastened to him to thank and bless him for his prophetic and beneficent aid.

Often he himself accompanied them in their voyages of circumnavigation or exploration, and paid many visits to the isles of the Hebridean archipelago discovered or frequented by the sailors of his community, and where *cells* or little colonies from the great island monastery seem to have existed. This was specially the case at Eigg, where a colony of fifty-two monks, founded and ruled by a disciple of the abbot of Iona, were killed by pirates twenty years after his death. This was a favourite spot which he loved to visit, no doubt to enjoy the solitude which was no longer to be found at Iona, where the crowds of penitents, pilgrims, and petitioners increased from day to day. And he took special pleasure also in Skye, the largest of the Hebridean isles, which, after the elapse of twelve centuries, was recalled to the attention of the world by the dangerous and romantic adventures of Prince Charles-Edward and Flora Macdonald. It was then scarcely inhabited, though very large and covered by forests, in which he could bury himself and pray, leaving even his brethren far behind him. One day he met an immense wild boar pursued by dogs; with a single word he killed the ferocious brute, instead of protecting it, as in similar cases the saints of the Merovingian legends were so ready to do. He continued during all the middle ages the patron of Skye, where a little lake still bears his name, as well as several spots and monuments in the neighbouring isles.

Storms often disturbed these excursions by sea,

and then Columba showed himself as laborious and bold as the most tried of his monastic mariners. When all were engaged in rowing, he would not remain idle, but rowed with them. We have seen him brave the frequent storms of the narrow and dangerous lakes in the north of Scotland. At sea he retained the same courageous composure in the most tempestuous weather, and took part in all the sailors' toils. During the voyage which he made from Iona to Ireland, to attend with King Aïdan the parliament of Drumceitt, his vessel was in great danger; the waves dashed into the boat till it was full of water, and Columba took his part with the sailors in baling it out. But his companions stopped him. "What you are doing at present is of little service to us," they said to him; "you would do better to pray for those who are about to perish." He did so, and the sea grew calm from the moment when, mounting on the prow, he raised his arms in prayer.

With these examples before them, his companions naturally appealed to his intercession whenever storms arose during any of his voyages. On one occasion he answered them, "It is not my turn; it is the holy abbot Kenneth who must pray for us." Kenneth was the abbot of a monastery in Ireland, and a friend of Columba's who came often to Iona to visit him. At the very same hour he heard the voice of his friend echo in his heart, and, warned by an internal voice, left the refectory where he was, and hastened to the church to pray for the shipwrecked, crying, "We have something else to do than to dine when Columba is in danger of perishing at sea." He did not even take the time to put on both his shoes before he went to the church, for which he received the special thanks of his friend at Iona; an incident which recalls another Celtic legend—that of the bishop St Paternus, who obeyed the call of his metropolitan with a boot upon one foot only.

Under all these legendary digressions it is evident that the monastic apostle of Caledonia, apart from the prevailing efficacy of his prayers, had made an attentive study of the winds and of all the phenomena of nature which affected the lives of the insular and maritime people whom he sought to lead into Christianity. A hundred different narratives represent him to us as the Eolus of those fabulous times and dangerous seas. He was continually entreated to grant a favourable wind for such or such an expedition; it even happened one day that two of his monks, on the eve of setting out in two different directions, came to him to ask, the one a north wind, and the other a south wind. He granted the prayer of both, but by delaying the departure of the one who was going to Ireland until after the arrival of the other, who went only to the neighbouring isle of Tiree.

Thus it happened that from far and near Columba was invoked or feared by the sailors as the master of all the winds that blew. Libran of the Rushes, the generous penitent whose curious history has been already recorded, wishing to return from Ireland to Iona, was turned back by the crew of the boat which was leaving the port of Derry for Scotland, because he was not a member of the community of Iona. Upon which the disappointed traveller mentally invoked across the sea the help of his absent friend. The wind immediately changed, and the boat was driven back to land. The sailors saw poor Libran still lingering upon the shore, and called to him from the deck, "Perhaps it is because of thee that the wind has changed; if we take thee with us, art thou disposed to make it once more favourable?" "Yes," said the monk; "the holy abbot Columba, who imposed upon me seven years of penitence, whom I have obeyed, and to whom I wish to return, will obtain that grace for you." And the result was that he was taken on board, and the journey was happily accomplished.

These events took place in his lifetime; but during at least a century after his death he remained the patron, always popular and propitious, of sailors in danger. A tone of familiar confidence, and sometimes of filial objurgation, may be remarked in their prayers, such as may be found among the Celts of Armorica and the Catholic nations of the south of Europe. Adamnan confesses that he himself and some other monks of Iona, embarked in a flotilla of a dozen boats charged with oaken beams for the reconstruction of the monastery, were so detained by contrary winds in a neighbouring island, that they took to accusing their Columba. "Dear saint," they said to him, "what dost thou think of this delay? We thought up to this moment that thou hadst great favour with God." Another time, when they were detained by the same cause in a bay near the district of Lorn, precisely on the vigil of St Columba's day, they said to him, "How canst thou leave us to pass thy feast to-morrow among laymen, and not in thine own church? It would be so easy for thee to obtain from the Lord that this contrary wind should become favourable, and permit us to sing mass in thy church!" On these two occasions their desires were granted; the wind changed suddenly, and permitted them to get to sea and make their way to Iona in those frail boats whose spars, crossing upon the mast, formed the august symbol of redemption. More than a hundred witnesses of these facts were still living when the biographer of our saint wrote his history.

This tender and vigilant charity, which lent itself to all the incidents of a sailor's and traveller's life, becomes still more strongly apparent during all the phases of his existence, in his relations with the agricultural population, whether of Ireland, which was his cradle, or of his adopted country Caledonia. Amid the fabulous legends and apocryphal and childish miracles with which Irish historians have filled out the glorious story of the great missionary, it is pleasant to be able to discover the unmistakable evidence of his intelligent and fruitful solicitude for the necessities, the labours, and the sufferings of the inhabitants of the rural districts, and his active intervention on their behalf. When the legend tells us how, with one stroke of his crosier, he made fountains of sweet waters spring in a hundred different corners of Ireland or Scotland, in arid and rocky districts, such as that of the peninsula of Ardnamurchan; when it shows him lowering, by his prayers, the cataracts of a river so that the salmon could ascend in the fishing season, as they have always done since, to the great benefit of the dwellers by the stream, we recognise in the tale the most touching expression of popular and national gratitude for the services which the great monk rendered to the country, by teaching the peasants to search for the fountains, to regulate the irrigations, and to rectify the course of the rivers, as so many other holy monks have done in all European lands.

It is equally apparent that he had with zeal and success established the system of grafting and the culture of fruit-trees, when we read the legend which represents him to us, at the beginning of his monastic career in Durrow, the most ancient of his foundations, approaching, in autumn, a tree covered with sour and unwholesome fruit, to bless it, and saying, "In the name of Almighty God, let thy bitterness leave thee, O bitter tree, and let thy apples be henceforward as sweet as up to this time they have been sour!" At other times he is said to have obtained for his friends quick and abundant harvests, enabling them, for example, to cut barley in August which they had sown in June—a thing which then seemed a miracle, but is not without parallel in Scotland at the present time. Thus almost invariably the recollection of a service rendered, or of a benefit asked or spontaneously conferred, weds itself in the legend to the story of miracles and outbursts of wonder-working prayer—which, in most cases, were for the benefit of the cultivators of the soil: it is evident that he studied their necessities and followed their vicissitudes with untiring sympathy.

In the same spirit he studied and sought remedies for the infectious diseases which threatened life, or which made ravages among the cattle of the country. Seated one day upon a hillock in his island, he said to the monk who was with him, and who belonged to the Dalriadian colony, "Look at that thick and rainy cloud which comes from the north; it has within it the germs of a deadly sickness; it is about to fall upon a large district of our Ireland, bringing ulcers and sores upon the body of man and beast. We must have pity on our brethren. Quick, let us go down, and to-morrow thou shalt embark and go to their aid." The monk obeyed, and, furnished with bread which Columba had blessed, he went over all the district smitten by the pestilence, distributing to the first sick persons he met, water, in which the bread blessed by the exiled abbot, who concerned himself so anxiously about the lot of his countrymen, had been steeped. The remedy worked so well, that from all parts both men and beasts crowded round the messenger of Iona, and the praises of Christ and His servant Columba resounded far and wide.

Thus we see the saint continually on the watch for those evils, losses, and accidents which struck the families or nations specially interesting to him, and which were revealed to him either by a supernatural intuition or by some plaintive appeal. Sometimes we find him sending the blessed bread, which was his favourite remedy, to a holy girl who had broken her leg in returning from mass; sometimes curing others of ophthalmia by means of salt also blessed; everywhere on his evangelical journeys, or other expeditions, we are witnesses of his desire, and the pains he took, to heal all the sick that were brought to him, or who awaited him on the roadside, eager, like the little idiot of Clonmacnoise, to touch the border of his robe—an accompaniment which had followed him during the whole course of his journey to the national assembly of Drumceitt.

His entire life bears the mark of his ardent sympathy for the labourers in the fields. From the time of his early travels as a young man in Ireland, when he furnished the ploughmen with ploughshares, and had the young men trained to the trade of blacksmith, up to the days of his old age, when he could only follow far off the labour of his monks, his paternal tenderness never ceased to exercise on their account its salutary and beneficent influence. Seated in the little wooden hut which answered the purpose of a cell, he interrupted his studies, and put down his pen, to bless the monks as they came back from the fields, the pastures, or the barns. The younger brethren, after having milked the cows of the community, knelt down, with their pails full of new milk, to receive from a distance the abbot's blessing, sometimes accompanied by an exhortation useful to their souls. During one of the last summers of his life, the monks, returning in the evening from reaping the scanty harvest of their island, stopped short as they approached the monastery, suddenly touched with strange emotion. The steward of the monastery, Baithen, the friend and future successor of Columba, asked them, "Are you not sensible of something very unusual here?" "Yes," said the oldest of the monks, "every day, at this hour and place, I breathe a delicious odour, as if all the flowers in the world were collected here. I feel also something like the flame of the hearth which does not burn but warms me gently; I experience, in short, in my heart a joy so unusual, so incomparable, that I am no longer sensible of either trouble or fatigue. The sheaves which I carry on my back, though heavy, weigh upon me no longer; and I know not how, from this spot to the monastery, they seem to be lifted from my shoulders. What, then, is this wonder?" All the others gave the same account of their sensations. "I will tell you what it is," said the steward; "it is our old master, Columba, always full of anxiety for us, who is disturbed to find us so late, who vexes himself with the thought of our fatigue, and who, not being able to come to meet us with his body, sends us his spirit to refresh, rejoice, and console us."

It must not be supposed, however, that he reserved his solicitude for his monastic labourers alone. Far from that, he knew how to appreciate the work of laymen when sanctified by Christian virtue. "See," he said one day to the elders of the monastery, "at this moment while I speak, such a one who was a blacksmith yonder in Ireland—see him, how he goes up to heaven! He dies an old man, and he has worked all his life; but he has not worked in vain. He has bought eternal life with the work of his hands; for he dispensed all his gains in alms; and I see the angels who are going for his soul." It will be admitted that the praise of manual labour, carried to a silly length in our days, has been rarely expressed in a manner so solemn and touching.

It is also recorded that he took pleasure in the society of laymen during his journeys, and lived among them with a free and delightful familiarity.

This is one of the most attractive and instructive phases of his history. He continually asked and received the hospitality not only of the rich, but also of the poor; and sometimes, indeed, received a more cordial reception from the poor than from the rich. To those who refused him a shelter he predicted prompt punishment. "That miser," he said, "who despises Christ in the person of a traveller, shall see his wealth diminish from day to day and come to nothing; he will come to beggary, and his son shall go from door to door holding out his hand, which shall never be more than half filled." When the poor received him under their roof, he inquired with his ordinary thoughtfulness into their resources, their necessities, all their little possessions. At that period a man seems to have been considered very poor in Scotland who had only five cows. This was all the fortune of a Lochaber peasant in whose house Columba, who continually traversed this district when going to visit the king of the Picts, passed a night, and found a very cordial welcome notwithstanding the poverty of the house. Next morning he had the five little cows brought into his presence and blessed them, predicting to his host that he should soon have five hundred, and that the blessing of the grateful missionary should go down to his children and grandchildren—a prophecy which was faithfully fulfilled.

In the same district of Lochaber, which is still the scene of those great deer-stalking expeditions in which the British aristocracy delight, our saint was one day accosted by an unfortunate poacher, who had not the means of maintaining his wife and children, and who asked alms from him. "Poor man," said Columba, "go and cut me a rod in the forest." When the rod was brought to him, the abbot of Iona himself sharpened it into the form of a spear. When he had done this he blessed the improvised javelin, and gave it to his suppliant, telling him that if he kept it carefully, and used it only against wild beasts, venison should never be wanting in his poor house. This prophecy also was fulfilled. The poacher planted his blessed spear in a distant corner of the forest, and no day passed that he did not find there a hart or doe, or other game, so that he soon had enough to sell to his neighbours as well as to provide for all the necessities of his own house.

Columba thus interested himself in all that he saw, in all that went on around him, and which he could turn to the profit of the poor or of his fellow-creatures; even in hunting or fishing he took pains to point out the happy moment and most favourable spot where the largest salmon or pike might be found. Wherever he found himself in contact with the poor or with strangers, he drew them to himself and comforted them even more by the warm sympathy of his generous heart than by material benefits. He identified himself with their fears, their dangers, and their vexations. Always a peacemaker and consoler, he took advantage here of the night's shelter given him by a rich mountaineer to end a dispute between two angry neighbours; and there made a chance meeting in a Highland gorge with a countryman an occasion for reassuring the peasant as to the consequences of the ravages made in his district by Pictish or Saxon invaders. "My good man," he said, "thy poor cattle and thy little all have fallen into the hands of the robbers; but thy dear little family is safe—go home and be comforted."

Such was this tender and gentle soul. His charity might sometimes seem to have degenerated into feebleness, so great was the pleasure he took in all the details of benevolence and Christian brotherhood; but let there appear an injustice to repair, an unfortunate individual to defend, an oppressor to punish, an outrage against humanity or misfortune to avenge, and Columba immediately awoke and displayed all the energy of his youth. The former man reappeared in a moment; his passionate temperament recovered the mastery—his distinctive character, vehement in expression and resolute in action, burst forth at every turn; and his natural boldness led him, in the face of all dangers, to lavish remonstrances, invectives, and threats, which the justice of God, too rarely visible in such cases, sometimes deigned to fulfil.

Among the many sufferers whom he found on his way, it is natural to suppose that the exiles, who were so numerous in consequence of the discords which rent the Celtic races, would most of all call forth his sympathy. Himself an exile, he was the natural protector of all who were exiled. He took under his special guardianship a banished Pict, of noble family, probably one of those who had received him with kindness and listened to his teachings at the time of his first missions in Northern Caledonia. Columba confided, or, as the historian says, recommended, assigned *in manum*, according to the custom which came to be general in feudal times, his banished friend to a chief called Feradagh, who occupied the large island of Islay, south of Iona, praying him to conceal his guest for some months among his clan and dependants. A few days after he had solemnly accepted the trust, this villain had the noble exile treacherously murdered, no doubt for the sake of the articles of value he had with him. When he received the news, Columba cried, "It is not to me, it is to God, that this wretched man, whose name shall be effaced out of the book of life, has lied. It is summer now, but before autumn comes—before he can eat of the meat which he is fattening for his table—he shall die a sudden death, and be dragged to hell." The indignant old man's prophecy was reported to Feradagh, who pretended to laugh at it, but nevertheless kept it in his mind. Before the beginning of autumn, he ordered a fattened pig to be killed and roasted, and even before the animal was entirely cooked gave orders that part of it should be served to him, in order to prove, at the earliest possible moment, the falsehood of the prophesied vengeance. But scarcely had he taken up the morsel, when, before he had carried it to his mouth, he fell back and died. Those who were present admired and trembled to see how the Lord God honoured and justified his prophet; and those who knew Columba's life as a young man recalled to each other how, at the very beginning of his monastic life, the murderer of the innocent maiden had fallen dead at the sound of his avenging voice.

In his just wrath against the spoilers of the poor and the persecutors of the Church, he drew back before no danger, not even before the assassin's dagger. Among the rievers who infested Scottish Caledonia, making armed incursions into their neighbours' lands, and carrying on that system of pillage which, up to the eighteenth century, continued to characterise the existence of the Scottish clans, he had distinguished the sons of Donnell, who belonged to a branch of the family which ruled the Dalriadian colony. Columba did not hesitate to excommunicate them. Exasperated by this sentence, one of these powerful ill-doers, named or surnamed Lamm-Dess (*Right-hand*), took advantage of a visit which the great abbot paid to a distant island, and undertook to murder him in his sleep. But Finn-Lugh, one of the saint's companions, having had some suspicion or instinctive presentiment of danger, and desiring to save his father's life by the sacrifice of his own, borrowed Columba's cowl, and wrapped himself in it. The assassin struck him whom he found clothed in the well-known costume of the abbot, and then fled. But the sacred vestment proved impenetrable armour to the generous disciple, who was not even wounded. Columba, when informed of the event, said nothing at the moment. But a year after, when he had returned to Iona, the abbot said to his community, "A year ago Lamm-Dess did his best to murder my dear Finn-Lugh in my place; now at this moment it is he who is being killed." And, in fact, the news shortly arrived that the assassin had just died under the sword of a warrior, who struck the fatal blow while invoking the name of Columba, in a fight which brought the depredations of these rievers to an end.

Some time before, another criminal of the same family, called Joan, had chosen for his victim one of the hosts of Columba, one of those poor men whom the abbot had enriched by his blessing in exchange for the hospitality which even in their poverty they had not refused. This poor man lived on the wild and barren peninsula of Ardnamurchan, a sombre mass which rises up out of the waves of the Atlantic, and forms the most western point of the Scottish mainland. The benediction of the missionary had brought him good fortune, as had been the case with the peasant of Lochaber, and his five cows, too, had multiplied, and were then more than a hundred in number. Columba was not satisfied with merely enriching his humble friend, but gave him also a place in his affections, and had even bestowed upon him his own name; so that all his neighbours called him *Columbain*, the friend of St Columba. Three times in succession, Joan, the princely spoiler, had pillaged and ravaged the house of the enriched peasant, the friend of the abbot of Iona; the third time, as he went back with his bravos, laden with booty, to the boat which awaited him on the beach, he met the great abbot, whom he had supposed far distant. Columba reproved him for his exactions and crimes, and entreated him to give up his prey; but the riever continued his course, and answered only by an immovable silence, until he had gained the beach and entered his boat. As soon as he was in his vessel, he began to answer the abbot's prayers by mockeries and insults. Then the noble old man plunged into the sea, up to his knees, as if to cling to the boat which contained the spoils of his friend; and when it went off he remained for some time with his two hands raised towards heaven, praying with ardour. When his prayer was ended, he came out of the water, and returned to his companions, who were seated on a neighbouring mound, to dry himself. After a pause, he said to them, "This miserable man, this evil-doer, who despises Christ in His servants, shall never more land upon the shore from which you have seen him depart—he shall never touch land again. To-day a little cloud begins to rise in the north, and from that cloud comes a tempest that shall swallow him up, him and his; not one single soul shall escape to tell the tale." The day was fine, the sea calm, and the sky perfectly serene. Notwithstanding, the cloud which Columba had announced soon appeared; and the spectators, turning their eyes to the sea, saw the tempest gather, increase, and pursue the spoilers. The storm reached them between the islands of Mull and Colonsay, from whose shores their boat was seen to sink and perish, with all its crew and all its spoils.

We have all read in Cæsar's Commentaries how, when he landed on the shores of Britain, the standard-bearer of the tenth legion threw himself into the sea, up to the knees in water, to encourage his comrades. Thanks to the perverse complaisance of history for all feats of force, this incident is immortal. Cæsar, however, moved by depraved ambition, came but to oppress a free and innocent race, and to bring it under the odious yoke of Roman tyranny, of which, happily, it has retained no trace. How much grander and more worthy of recollection, I do not say to every Christian, but to every upright soul, is the sight offered to us at the other extremity of the great Britannic Isle, by this old monk, who also rushed into the sea up to his knees—but to pursue a savage oppressor, in the interest of an obscure victim, thus claiming for himself, under his legendiary aureola, the everlasting greatness of humanity, justice, and pity!

CHAPTER VII.

Columba's last Years—His Death—His Character.

BY the side of the terrible acts of vengeance which have just been narrated, the student loves to find in this bold enemy of the wicked and the oppressor a gentle and familiar sympathy for all the affections as well as all the trials of domestic life. Rich and poor, kings and peasants, awoke in his breast the same kindly emotion, expressed with the same fulness. When King Aïdan brought his children to him, and spoke of his anxiety about their future lives, he did not content himself with seeing the eldest. "Have you none younger?" said the abbot; "bring them all—let me hold them in my arms and on my heart!" And when the younger children were wrought, one fair-haired boy, Hector (Eochaidh Buidhe), came forward running, and threw himself upon the saint's knees. Columba held him long pressed to his heart, then kissed his forehead, blessed him, and prophesied for him a long life, a prosperous reign, and a great posterity.

Let us listen while his biographer tells how he came to the aid of a woman in extremity, and how he made peace in a divided household. One day at Iona he suddenly stopped short while reading, and said with a smile to his monks, "I must now go and pray for a poor little woman who is in the pains of childbirth, and suffers like a true daughter of Eve. She is down yonder in Ireland, and reckons upon my prayers, for she is my kinswoman, and of my mother's family." Upon this he hastened to the church, and when his prayer was ended returned to his brethren, saying, "She is delivered. The Lord Jesus, who deigned to be born of a woman, has come to her aid; this time she will not die."

Another day, while he was visiting an island on the Irish coast, a pilot came to him to complain of his wife, who had taken an aversion to him. The abbot called her and reminded her of the duties imposed upon her by the law of the Lord. "I am ready to do everything," said the woman—"I will obey you in the hardest things you can command. I do not draw back from any of the cares of the house. I will go even, if it is desired, on pilgrimage to Jerusalem, or I will shut myself up in a nunnery — in short, I will do everything except live with him."

The abbot answered that there could be no question of pilgrimage or of a convent so long as her husband lived; "but," he added, "let us try to pray God, all three, fasting—you, your husband, and myself."

"Ah," said the woman, "I know that you can obtain even what is impossible from God." However, his proposal was carried out—the three fasted, and Columba passed the whole night in prayer without ever closing his eyes. Next morning he said to the woman, with the gentle irony which he so often employed, "Tell me to what convent are you bound after your yesterday's projects?" "To none," said the woman; "my heart has been changed to-night. I know not how I have passed from hate to love." And from that day until the hour of her death she lived in a tender and faithful union with her husband.

But Columba fortunately was connected with other households more united, where he could admire the happiness of his friends without feeling himself compelled to make peace. From his sanctuary at Iona his habitual solicitude and watchful sympathy followed them to their last hour. One day he was alone with one of the Saxons whom he had converted and attached to his community, and who was the baker of the monks; while this stranger prepared his bread, he heard the abbot say, looking up to heaven, "Oh! happy, happy woman! She goes into heaven with a guard of angels."

Exactly a year after, the abbot and the Saxon baker were again together. "I see the woman," said Columba, "of whom I spoke to thee last year coming down from heaven to meet the soul of her husband, who has just died. She contends with powerful enemies for that dear soul, by the help of the holy angels: she gains the day, she triumphs, because her goodman has been a just man—and the two are united again in the home of everlasting consolation."

This vision was preceded and followed by many others of the same description, in which the blessed death of many bishops and monks, his friends and contemporaries, were announced to him. They seem to have been intended to give him a glimpse of that heaven into which God was shortly to call him. Nor was it only at Iona that these supernatural graces were accorded to him, for he did not limit his unwearied activity to the narrow enclosure of that island, any more in the decline of his life than in the earlier period of his emigration. Up to old age he continued to have sufficient strength and courage to return to the most northern regions where he had preached the faith to the Picts; and it was in one of his last missionary journeys, when upon the banks of Loch Ness, to the north of the great line of waters which cuts Caledonia in two, at a distance of fifty leagues from Iona, that he was permitted to see the angels come to meet the soul of the old Pict, who, faithful during all his life to the law of nature, received baptism, and with it eternal salvation, from the great missionary's hands.

At this period the angels, whom he saw carrying to heaven the soul of the just and penitent, and aiding the believing wife to make an entrance there for her husband, continually appeared to him and hovered about him. Making all possible allowance for the exaggerations and fables which the proverbial credulity of Celtic nations has added to the legends of their saints, no Christian will be tempted to deny the verified narratives which bear witness, in Columba's case as well as in that of the other saints, to supernatural appearances which enriched his life, and especially his old age. Those wonderful soldiers of virtue and Christian truth needed such miracles to help them to support the toils and live through the trials of their dangerous mission. They required to ascend from time to time into celestial regions to find strength there for their continual struggle against all obstacles and perils and continually renewed temptations— and to learn to brave the enmities, the savage manners, and blind hatreds of the nations whom it was the aim of their lives to set free.

"Let no one follow me to-day," Columba said one morning with unusual severity to the assembled community: "I would be alone in the little plain to the west of the isle." He was obeyed; but a brother, more curious and less obedient than the rest, followed him far off, and saw him, erect and motionless, with his hands and his eyes raised to heaven, standing on a sandy hillock, where he was soon surrounded by a crowd of angels, who came to bear him company and to talk with him. The hillock has to this day retained the name of *Cnocan Aingel*—the Angels' Hill. And the citizens of the celestial country, as they were called at Iona, came often to console and strengthen their future companion during the long winter nights which he passed in prayer in some retired corner, voluntarily exposed to all the torments of sleeplessness and cold.

For as he approached the end of his career this great servant of God consumed his strength in vigils, fasts, and dangerous macerations. His life, which had been so full of generous struggles, hard trial, and toil in the service of God and his neighbour, seemed to him neither full enough nor pure enough. In proportion as the end drew near he redoubled his austerities and mortifications. Every night, according to one of his biographers, he plunged into cold water and remained there for the time necessary to recite an entire psalter. One day, when, bent by age, he sought, perhaps in a neighbouring island, a retirement still more profound than usual, in which to pray, he saw a poor woman gathering wild herbs and even nettles, who told him that her poverty was such as to forbid her all other food. Upon which the old abbot reproached himself bitterly that he had not yet come to that point. "See," he said, "this poor woman, who finds her miserable life worth the trouble of being thus prolonged; and we, who profess to deserve heaven by our austerities, we live in luxury!" When he went back to his monastery he gave orders that he should be served with no other food than the wild and bitter herbs with which the beggar supported her existence; and he severely reproved his minister, Diarmid, who had come from Ireland with him, when he, out of compassion for his master's old age and weakness, threw a little butter into the caldron in which this miserable fare was cooked.

The celestial light which was soon to receive him began already to surround him like a garment or a shroud. His monks told each other that the solitary cell in the isle of Himba, near Iona, which he had built for himself, was lighted up every night by a great light, which could be seen through the chinks of the door and keyhole, while the abbot chanted unknown canticles till daybreak. After having remained there three days and nights without food, he came out, full of joy at having discovered the mysterious meaning of several texts of Holy Scripture, which up to that time he had not understood. When he returned to Iona to die, continuing faithful to his custom of spending a great part of the night in prayer, he bore about with him everywhere the miraculous light which already surrounded him like the nimbus of his holiness. The entire community was involuntarily agitated by the enjoyment of that foretaste of paradise. One winter's night, a young man who was destined to succeed Columba as fourth abbot of Iona remained in the church while the others slept: all at once he saw the abbot come in preceded by a golden light which fell from the heights of the vaulted roof, and lighted all the corners of the building, even including the little lateral oratory where the young monk hid himself in alarm. All who passed during the night before the church, while their old abbot prayed, were startled by this light, which dazzled them like lightning. Another of the young monks, whose education was specially directed by the abbot himself, resolved to ascertain whether the same illumination existed in Columba's cell; and notwithstanding that he had been expressly forbidden to do so, he got up in the night and went groping to the door of the cell to look in, but fled immediately, blinded by the light that filled it.

These signs, which were the forerunners of his deliverance, showed themselves for several years towards the end of his life, which he believed and hoped was nearer its termination than it proved to be. But this remnant of existence, from which he sighed to be liberated, was held fast by the filial love of his disciples, and the ardent prayers of so many new Christian communities founded or ministered to by his zealous care. Two of his monks, one Irish and one Saxon, of the number of those whom he admitted to his cell to help him in his labour or to execute his instructions, saw him one day change countenance, and perceived in his face a sudden expression of the most contrary emotions: first a beatific joy, which made him raise to heaven a look full of the sweetest and tenderest gratitude; but a minute after this ray of supernatural joy gave place to an expression of heavy and profound sadness. The two spectators pressed him with questions which he refused to answer. At length they threw themselves at his knees, and begged him, with tears, not to afflict them by hiding what had been revealed to him. "Dear children," he said to them, "I do not wish to afflict you. . . . Know, then, that it is thirty years to-day since I began my pilgrimage in Caledonia. I have long prayed God to let my exile end with this thirtieth year, and to recall me to the heavenly country. When you saw me so joyous, it was because I could already see the angels who came to seek my soul. But all at once they stopped short, down there upon that rock at the farthest limit of the sea which surrounds our island, as if they would approach to take me, and could not. And, in truth, they could not, because the Lord has paid less regard to my ardent prayer than to that of the many churches which have prayed for me, and which have obtained, against my will, that I should still dwell in this body for four years. This is the reason of my sadness. But in four years I shall die without being sick; in four years, I know it and see it, they will come back, these holy angels, and I shall take my flight with them towards the Lord."

At the end of the four years thus fixed he arranged everything for his departure. It was the end of May, and it was his desire to take leave of the monks who worked in the fields in the only fertile part of Iona, the western side. His great age prevented him from walking, and he was drawn in a car by oxen. When he reached the labourers he said to them, "I greatly desired to die a month ago, on Easter-day, and it was granted to me; but I preferred to wait a little longer, in order that the festival might not be changed into a day of sadness for you." And when all wept he did all he could to console them. Then turning towards the east, from the top of his rustic chariot he blessed the island and all its inhabitants—a blessing which, according to local tradition, was like that of St Patrick in Ireland, and drove, from that day, all vipers and venomous creatures out of the island.

On Saturday in the following week he went, leaning on his faithful attendant Diarmid, to bless the granary of the monastery. Seeing there two great heaps of corn, the fruit of the last harvest, he said, "1 see with joy that my dear monastic family, if 1 must leave them this year, will not at least suffer from famine." "Dear father," said Diarmid, "why do you thus sadden us by talking of your death?" "Ah, well," said the abbot, "here is a little secret which I will tell thee if thou wilt swear on thy knees to tell no one before I am gone. To-day is Saturday, the day which the Holy Scriptures call Sabbath or rest. And it will be truly my day of rest, for it shall be the last of my laborious life. This very night I shall enter into the path of my fathers. Thou weepest, dear Diarmid, but console thyself; it is my Lord Jesus Christ who deigns to invite me to rejoin Him; it is He who has revealed to me that my summons will come to-night."

Then he left the storehouse to return to the monastery, but when he had gone half-way stopped to rest at a spot which is still marked by one of the ancient crosses of Iona—the monument called Maclean's Cross. At this moment an ancient and faithful servant, the old white horse which had been employed to carry milk from the dairy daily to the monastery, came towards him. He came and put his head upon his master's shoulder, as if to take leave of him. The eyes of the old horse had an expression so pathetic that they seemed to be bathed in tears. Diarmid would have sent the animal away, but the good old man forbade him. "The horse loves me," he said, "leave him with me; let him weep for my departure. The Creator has revealed to this poor animal what He has hidden from thee, a reasonable man." Upon which, still caressing the faithful brute, he gave him a last blessing. When this was done he used the remnants of his strength to climb to the top of a hillock from which he could see all the isle and the monastery, and there lifted up his hands to pronounce a prophetic benediction on the sanctuary he had created. "This little spot, so small and low, shall be greatly honoured, not only by the Scots kings and people, but also by foreign chiefs and barbarous nations; and it shall be venerated even by the saints of other Churches."

After this he went down to the monastery, entered his cell, and began to work for the last time. He was then occupied in transcribing the Psalter. When he had come to the 33d Psalm and the verse, *Inquirentes autem Dominum non deficient omni bono*, he stopped short. "I must stop here," he said; "Baithen will write the rest." Baithen, as has been seen, was the steward of Iona, and was to become its abbot. After this the aged saint was present at the vigil service before Sunday in the church. When he returned to his cell he seated himself upon the naked stones which served the septuagenarian for bed and pillow, and which were shown for nearly a century near his tomb. Then he intrusted to his only companion a last message for the community: "Dear children, this is what I command with my last words—let peace and charity, a charity mutual and sincere, reign always among you! If you act thus, following the example of the saints, God who strengthens the just will help you, and I, who shall be near Him, will intercede on your behalf, and you shall obtain of Him not only all the necessities of the present life in sufficient quantity, but still more the rewards of eternal life, reserved for those who keep His law."

These were his last words. As soon as the midnight bell had rung for the matins of the Sunday festival, he rose and hastened before the other monks to the church, where he knelt down before the altar. Diarmid followed him, but as the church was not yet lighted he could only find him by groping and crying in a plaintive voice, "Where art thou, my father?" He found Columba lying before the altar, and, placing himself at his side, raised the old abbot's venerable head upon his knees. The whole community soon arrived with lights, and wept as one man at the sight of their dying father. Columba opened his eyes once more, and turned them to his children on either side with a look full of serene and radiant joy. Then with the aid of Diarmid he raised, as best he might, his right hand to bless them all; his hand dropped, the last sigh came from his lips; and his face remained calm and sweet like that of a man who in his sleep had seen a vision of heaven.

Such was the life and death of the first great apostle of Great Britain. We have lingered, perhaps, too long on the grand form of this monk, rising up before us from the midst of the Hebridean sea, who, for the third part of a century, spread over those sterile isles, and gloomy distant shores, a pure and fertilising light. In a confused age and unknown region he displayed all that is greatest and purest, and, it must be added, most easily forgotten, in human genius: the gift of ruling souls by ruling himself. To select the most marked and graphic incidents from the general tissue of his life, and those most fit to unfold that which attracts the modern reader—that is, his personal character and influence upon contemporary events—from a world of minute details having almost exclusive reference to matters supernatural or ascetical, has been no easy task. But when this is done, it becomes comparatively easy to represent to ourselves the tall old man, with his fine and regular features, his sweet and powerful voice, the Irish tonsure high on his shaven head, and his long locks falling behind, clothed with his monastic cowl, and seated at the prow of his coracle, steering through the misty archipelago and narrow lakes of the north of Scotland, and bearing from isle to isle and from shore to shore, light, justice, and truth, the life of the conscience and of the soul.

One loves above all to study the depths of that soul, and the changes which had taken place in it since its youth. No more than his namesake of Luxeuil, the monastic apostle of Burgundy, was he of the Picts and Scots a *Columba*. Gentleness was of all qualities precisely the one in which he failed the most. At the beginning of his life the future abbot of Iona showed himself still more than the abbot of Luxeuil to be animated by all the vivacities of his age, associated with all the struggles and discords of his race and country. He was vindictive, passionate, bold, a man of strife, born a soldier rather than a monk, and known, praised, and blamed as a soldier—so that even in his lifetime he was invoked in fight; and continued a soldier, *insulanus miles*, even upon the island rock from which he rushed forth to preach, convert, enlighten, reconcile, and reprimand both princes and nations, men and women, laymen and clerks.

He was at the same time full of contradictions and contrasts—at once tender and irritable, rude and courteous, ironical and compassionate, caressing and imperious, grateful and revengeful—led by pity as well as by wrath, ever moved by generous passions, and among all passions fired to the very end of his life by two which his countrymen understand the best, the love of poetry and the love of country. Little inclined to melancholy when he had once surmounted the great sorrow of his life, which was his exile; little disposed even, save towards the end, to contemplation or solitude, but trained by prayer and austerities to triumphs of evangelical exposition; despising rest, untiring in mental and manual toil; born for eloquence, and gifted with a voice so penetrating and sonorous that it was thought of afterwards as one of the most miraculous gifts that he had received of God; frank and loyal, original and powerful in his words as in his actions—in cloister and mission and parliament, on land and on sea, in Ireland as in Scotland, always swayed by the love of God and of his neighbour, whom it was his will and pleasure to serve with an impassioned uprightness. Such was Columba. Besides the monk and missionary there was in him the makings of a sailor, soldier, poet, and orator. To us, looking back, he appears a personage as singular as he is lovable, in whom, through all the mists of the past and all the cross-lights of legend, the man may still be recognised under the saint—a man capable and worthy of the supreme honour of holiness, since he knew how to subdue his inclinations, his weakness, his instincts, and his passions, and to transform them into docile and invincible weapons for the salvation of souls and the glory of God.

CHAPTER VIII.

Spiritual Descendants of St Columba.

THE influence of Columba, as of all men really superior to their fellows, and especially of the saints, far from ceasing with his life, went on increasing after his death. The supernatural character of his virtues, the miracles which were attributed to his intercession with God, had for a long time left scarcely any doubt as to his sanctity. It was universally acknowledged after his death, and has since remained uncontested among all the Celtic races. The visions and miracles which went to prove it would fill a volume. On the night, and at the very hour, of his death, a holy old man in a distant monastery in Ireland, one of those whom the Celtic chroniclers call the victorious soldiers of Christ, saw with the eyes of his mind the isle of Iona, which he had never visited, flooded with miraculous light, and all the vault of heaven full of an innumerable army of shining angels, who went, singing celestial canticles, to bring away the holy soul of the great missionary. Upon the banks of a river, in Columba's native land, another holy monk, while occupied with several others in fishing, saw, as also did his companions, the sky lighted up by a pillar of fire, which rose from earth to the highest heaven, and disappeared only after lighting up the whole scene with a radiance as of the sun at noon.

Thus began the long succession of wonders by which the worship of Columba's holy memory is characterised among the Celtic races. This worship, which seemed at one time concentrated in one of the smallest islets of the Atlantic, extended in less than a century after his death, not only throughout all Ireland and Great Britain, but into Gaul, Spain, and Italy, and even to Rome, which some legends, insufficiently verified, describe him as having visited during the last years of his life, in order to renew the bonds of respectful affection and spiritual union which are supposed to have united him to the great pope St Gregory, who ascended the pontifical throne seven years before the death of the Hebridean apostle.

It was expected that all the population of the neighbouring districts would hasten to Iona and fill the island during the funeral of the great abbot; and this had even been intimated to him before he died. But he had prophesied that the fact would be otherwise, and that his monastic family alone should perform the ceremonies of his burial. And it happened, accordingly, during the three days which were occupied with those rites, that a violent wind made it impossible for any boat to reach the island. Thus this friend and counsellor of princes and nations, this great traveller, this apostle of an entire nation which, during a thousand years, was to honour him as its patron saint, lay solitary upon his bier, in the little church of his island retirement; and his burial was witnessed only by his monks. But his grave, though it was not dug in presence of an enthusiastic crowd, as had been looked for, was not the less visited and surrounded by floods of successive generations, who for more than two hundred years crowded there to venerate the relics of the holy missionary, and to drink the pure waters of his doctrine and example at the fountainhead.

The remains of Columba rested here in peace up to the ninth century, until the moment when Iona, like all the British isles, fell a prey to the ravages of the Danes. These cruel and insatiable pirates seem to have been attracted again and again by the wealth of the offerings that were lavished upon the tomb of the apostle of Caledonia. They burnt the monastery for the first time in 801; again in 805, when it contained only so small a number as sixty-four monks; and finally, a third time, in 877. To save from their rapacity a treasure which no pious liberality could replace, the body of St Columba was carried to Ireland. And it is the unvarying tradition of Irish annals that it was deposited finally at Down, in an episcopal monastery not far from the western shore of the island, between the great Monastery of Bangor on the north, from which came Columbanus of Luxeuil, and Dublin, the future capital of Ireland, to the south. There already lay the relics of Patrick and of Bridget; and thus was verified one of the prophecies in Irish verse attributed to Columba, in which he says—

> "They shall bury me first at Iona;
> But, by the will of the living God,
> It is at Dun that I shall rest in my grave,
> With Patrick and with Bridget the immaculate.
> Three bodies in one grave."

The three names have remained since that time inseparably united in the dauntless heart and fervent tenacious memory of the Irish people. It is to Columba that the oppressed and impoverished Irish seem to have appealed with the greatest confidence in the first English conquest in the twelfth century. The conquerors themselves feared him, not without reason, for they had learned to know his vengeance. John de Courcy, a warlike Anglo-Norman baron, he who was called the Conqueror (*Conquestor*) of Ulster, as William of Normandy of England, carried always with him the volume of Columba's prophecies; and when the bodies of the three saints were found in his new possessions.

in 1180, he prayed the Holy See to celebrate their translation by the appointment of a solemn festival. Richard Strongbow, the famous Earl of Pembroke, who had been the first chief of the invasion, died of an ulcer in the foot, which had been inflicted upon him, according to the Irish narrative, at the prayer of St Bridget, St Columba, and other saints, whose churches he had destroyed. He himself said, when at the point of death, that he saw the sweet and noble Bridget lift her arm to pierce him to the heart. Hugh de Lacy, another Anglo-Norman chief of great lineage, perished at Durrow, "by the vengeance of Columb-cille," says a chronicler, while he was engaged in building a castle to the injury of the abbey which Columba had founded, and loved so much. A century after, this *vengeance* was still popularly dreaded; and some English pirates, who had pillaged his church in the island of Inchcolm, having sunk like lead in sight of land, their countrymen said that he should be called, not St Columba, but St *Quhalme**—that is to say, the Saint of Sudden Death.

A nation has special need to believe in these vengeances of God, always so tardy and infrequent, and which, in Ireland, above all, have scarcely sufficed to light with a fugitive gleam the long night of the conquest, with all its iniquities and crimes. Happy are the people among whom the everlasting

---

* *Quhalme* in Anglo-Saxon meant sudden death, from whence the modern English word *qualm*.

justice of the appeal against falsehood and evil is placed under the shadow of God and the saints; and blessed also the saints who have left to posterity the memory of their indignation against all injustice.

As long as the body of Columba remained in his island grave, Iona, consecrated henceforward by the life and death of so great a Christian, continued to be the most venerated sanctuary of the Celts. For two centuries she was the nursery of bishops, the centre of education, the asylum of religious knowledge, the point of union among the British Isles, the capital and necropolis of the Celtic race. Seventy kings or princes were buried there at the feet of Columba, faithful to a kind of traditional law, the recollection of which has been consecrated by Shakespeare.* During these two centuries she retained an uncontested supremacy over all the monasteries and churches of Caledonia, as over those of half Ireland; and we shall hereafter see how she disputed with the Roman missionaries the authority over the Anglo-Saxons of the North. Later still, if we are permitted to follow this narrative so far, at the end of the eleventh century, we shall see her ruins raised up and restored to monastic life by one of the most noble and touching

* "ROSSE. Where is Duncan's body?
  MACDUFF. Carried to Colmes-Kill,
    The sacred storehouse of his predecessors,
    And guardian of their bones."
            SHAKESPEARE, *Macbeth.*

heroines of Scotland and Christendom, the holy Queen Margaret, the gentle and noble exile, so beautiful, so wise, so magnanimous and beloved, who used her influence over Malcolm her husband only for the regeneration of the Church in his kingdom, and whose dear memory is worthy of being associated in the heart of the Scottish people with that of Columba, since she obtained by his intercession that grace of maternity which has made her the origin of the dynasty which still reigns over the British Isles.

Let us here reconsider the privilege which gave to the abbots of Iona a sort of jurisdiction over the bishops of the neighbouring districts—a privilege unique, and which would even appear fabulous, if it were not attested by two of the most trustworthy historians of the time, the Venerable Bede and Notker of St Gall. In order to explain this strange anomaly, it must be understood that in Celtic countries, especially in Ireland and in Scotland, ecclesiastical organisation rested, in the first place, solely upon conventual life. Dioceses and parishes were regularly constituted only in the twelfth century. Bishops, it is true, existed from the beginning, but either without any clearly fixed territorial jurisdiction, or incorporated as a necessary but subordinate part of the ecclesiastical machinery with the great monastic bodies; and such was specially the case in Ireland. It is for this reason that the bishops of the Celtic Church, as has been often remarked, are so much overshadowed not only by great founders and superiors of monasteries, such as Columba, but even by simple abbots. Nevertheless, it is evident that during the life of Columba, far from assuming any superiority whatever over the bishops who were his contemporaries, he showed them the utmost respect, even to such a point that he would not celebrate mass in the presence of a bishop who had come, humbly disguised as a simple convert, to visit the community of Iona. At the same time the abbots scrupulously abstained from all usurpation of the rank, privileges, or functions reserved to bishops, to whom they had recourse for all the ordinations celebrated in the monasteries. But as most of the bishops had been educated in monastic schools, they retained an affectionate veneration for their cradle, which, in regard to Iona especially, from which we shall see so many bishops issue, might have translated itself into a sort of prolonged submission to the conventual authority of their former superior. Five centuries later the bishops who came from the great French abbeys of Cluny and Citeaux took pleasure in professing the same filial subordination to their monastic birthplace.

The uncontested primacy of Iona over the bishops who had there professed religion, or who came there to be consecrated after their election, may be besides explained by the influence exercised by Columba over both clergy and people of the districts evangelised by him—an influence which was only increased by his death.

Did the great abbot of Iona, like his namesake of Luxeuil, leave to his disciples a monastic rule of his own, distinct from that of other Celtic monasteries? This has been often asserted, but without positive proof—and in any case no authentic text of such a document exists. That which bears the name of the *Rule of Columb-kill*, and which has been sometimes attributed to him, has no reference in any way to the cenobites of Iona, and is only applicable to hermits or recluses, who lived perhaps under his authority, but isolated, and who were always very numerous in Ireland.

A conscientious and attentive examination of all the monastic peculiarities which can be discovered in his biography reveals absolutely nothing in respect to observances or obligations different from the rules borrowed by all the religious communities of the sixth century from the traditions of the Fathers of the Desert. Such an examination brings out distinctly, in the first place, the necessity for a vow or solemn profession to prove the final admission of the monk into the community after a probation more or less prolonged; and, in the second place, the absolute conformity of the monastic life of Columba and his monks to the precepts and rites of the Catholic Church in all ages. Authorities unquestionable and unquestioned demonstrate the existence of auricular confession, the invocation of saints, the universal faith in their protection and intervention in temporal affairs, the celebration of the mass, the real presence in the Eucharist, ecclesiastical celibacy, fasts and abstinences, prayer for the dead, the sign of the cross, and, above all, the assiduous and profound study of the Holy Scriptures. Thus the assumption made by certain writers of having found in the Celtic Church some sort of primitive Christianity not Catholic, crumbles to the dust ; and the ridiculous but inveterate prejudice which accuses our fathers of having ignored or interdicted the study of the Bible is once again proved to be without foundation.

As to the customs peculiar to the Irish Church, and which were afterwards the cause of so many tedious struggles with the Roman and Anglo-Saxon missionaries, no trace of them is to be discovered in the acts or words of Columba. There is no mention of the tiresome disputes about the tonsure, or even of the irregular celebration of Easter, except perhaps in a prophecy vaguely made by him on the occasion of a visit to Clonmacnoise, upon the discords which this difference of opinion in respect to Easter would one day excite in the Scotic Church.

If Columba made no rule calculated, like that of St Benedict, to last for centuries, he nevertheless left to his disciples a spirit of life, of union, and of discipline, which was sufficient to maintain in one great body, for several centuries after his death, not only the monks of Iona, but the numerous communities which had gathered round them. This monastic body bore a noble name; it was long called the Order of the Fair Company, and still longer the Family of Columb-kill. It was governed by abbots, who succeeded Columba as superiors of the community of Iona. These abbots proved themselves worthy of, and obtained from Bede, one of the most competent of judges, who began to write a hundred years after the death of Columba, a tribute of admiration without reserve, and even more striking than that which he gave to their founder:—" Whatever he may have been," said the Venerable Bede, with a certain shadow of Anglo-Saxon suspicion in respect to Celtic virtue and sanctity, "it is undeniable that he has left successors illustrious by the purity of their life, their great love of God, and their zeal for monastic order; and, although separated from us as to the observance of Easter, which is caused by their distance from all the rest of the world, ardently and closely devoted to the observance of those laws of piety and chastity which they have learned in the Old and New Testaments." These praises are justified by the great number of saints who have issued from the spiritual lineage of Columba; but they should be specially applied to his successors in the abbatial see of Iona, and, in the first place, to his first successor, whom he had himself pointed out, the holy and amiable Baithen, who was so worthy to be his lieutenant and friend, and could so well replace him. He survived Columba only three years, and died on the anniversary of his master's death. The cruel sufferings of his last illness did not prevent him from praying, writing, and teaching to his last hour. Baithen was, as has been said, the cousin-german of Columba, and almost all the abbots of Iona who succeeded him were of the same race.

The family spirit, or, to speak more truly, the clan spirit, always so powerful and active in Ireland, and which was so striking a feature in the character of Columba, had become a predominating influence in the monastic life of the Celtic Church. It was not precisely hereditary succession, since marriage was absolutely unknown among the regular clergy; but great influence was given to blood in the election of abbots, as in that of princes or military leaders. The nephew or cousin of the founder or superior of a monastery seemed the candidate pointed out by nature for the vacant dignity. Special reasons were necessary for breaking through this rule. Thus it is apparent that the eleven first abbots of Iona after Columba, proceeded, with the exception of one individual, from the same stock as himself, from the race of Tyrconnel, and were all descended from the same son of Niall of the Nine Hostages, the famous king of all Ireland. Every great monastery became thus the centre and appanage of a family, or, to speak more exactly, of a clan, and was alike the school and the asylum of all the founder's kindred. At a later period a kind of succession, purely laic and hereditary, developed itself by the side of the spiritual posterity, and was invested with the possession of most of the monastic domains. These two lines of descendants, simultaneous but distinct, from the principal monastic founders, are distinguished in the historical genealogies of Ireland under the names of *ecclesiastica progenies* and of *plebilis progenies*. After the ninth century, in consequence of the relaxation of discipline, the invasion of married clerks, and the increasing value of land, the line of spiritual descent confounded itself more and more with that of natural inheritance, and there arose a crowd of abbots purely lay and hereditary, as proud of being the collateral descendants of a holy founder, as they were happy to possess the vast domains with which the foundation had been gradually enriched. This fatal abuse made its appearance also in France and Germany, but was less inveterate than in Ireland, where it still existed in the time of St Bernard; and in Scotland, where it lasted even after the Reformation.

It was never thus at Iona, where the abbatical succession was always perfectly regular and uninterrupted up to the invasions and devastations of the Danes at the commencement of the eighth century. From the time of those invasions the abbots of Iona began to occupy an inferior position. The radiant centre from which Christian civilisation had shone upon the British Isles grew dim. The headquarters of the communities united under the title of the *Family* or *Order of Columb-kill*, were transferred from Iona to one of the other foundations of the saint at Kells, in the centre of Ireland, where a successor of Columba, superior-general of the order, titulary abbot of Iona, Armagh, or some other great Irish monastery, and bearing the distinctive title of *Coarb*, resided for three centuries more.

We have lingered too long over the great and touching figure of the saint whose life we have just recorded; and it now remains to us to throw a rapid glance at the influence which he exercised on all around him, and even upon posterity.

This influence is especially evident in the Irish Church, which seems to have been entirely swayed by his spirit, his successors, and his disciples, during the time which is looked upon as the Golden Age in its history, and which extends up to the period of the Danish invasions, at the end of the eighth century. During all this time the Irish Church, which continued, as from its origin, entirely monastic, seems to have been governed by the recollections or institutions of Columba. The words *Lex Columbcille* are found on many pages of its confused annals, and indicate sometimes the mass of traditions preserved by its monasteries, sometimes the tributes which the kings levied for the defence of the Church and country, while carrying through all Ireland the shrine which contained his relics. The continued influence of the great abbot of Iona was so marked, even in temporal affairs, that more than two centuries after his death, in 817, the monks of his order, *Congregatio Columbcille*, went solemnly to Tara, the ancient capital of Druidical Ireland, to excommunicate there the supreme monarch of the island, who had assassinated a prince of the family of their holy chief.

It has been said, and cannot be sufficiently repeated, that Ireland was then regarded by all Christian Europe as the principal centre of knowledge and piety. In the shelter of its numberless monasteries a crowd of missionaries, doctors, and preachers were educated for the service of the Church and the propagation of the faith in all Christian countries. A vast and continual development of literary and religious effort is there apparent, superior to anything that could be seen in any other country of Europe. Certain arts—those of architecture, carving, metallurgy, as applied to the decoration of churches — were successfully cultivated, without speaking of music, which continued to flourish both among the learned and among the people. The classic languages — not only Latin, but Greek—were cultivated, spoken, and written with a sort of passionate pedantry, which shows at least how powerful was the sway of intellectual influences over these ardent souls. Their mania for Greek was even carried so far that they wrote the Latin of the church books in Hellenic characters. And in Ireland more than anywhere else, each monastery was a school, and each school a workshop of transcription, from which day by day issued new copies of the Holy Scriptures and the Fathers of the primitive Church —copies which were dispersed through all Europe, and which are still to be found in Continental libraries. They may easily be recognised by the original and elegant character of their Irish writing, as also by the use of the alphabet common to all the Celtic races, and afterwards employed by the Anglo-Saxons, but to which in our day the Irish alone have remained faithful. Columba, as has been seen, had given an example of this unwearied labour to the monastic scribes; his example was continually followed in the Irish cloisters, where the monks did not entirely limit themselves to the transcription of Holy Scripture, but reproduced also Greek and Latin authors, sometimes in Celtic character, with gloss and commentary in Irish, like that Horace which modern learning has discovered in the library of Berne. These marvellous manuscripts, illuminated with incomparable ability and patience by the monastic family of Columba, excited, five hundred years later, the declamatory enthusiasm of a great enemy of Ireland, the Anglo-Norman historian, Gerald de Barry; and they still attract the attention of archæologists and philologists of the highest fame.

Exact annals of the events of the time were also made out in all the monasteries. These annals replaced the chronicles of the bards; and so far as they have been preserved, and already published or about to be so, they now form the principal source of Irish history. Ecclesiastical records have naturally a greater place in them than civil history. They celebrate especially the memory of the saints, who have always been so numerous in the Irish Church, where each of the great communities can count a circle of holy men, issued from its bosom or attached to its confraternity. Under the name of *sanctilogy* or *festilogy* (for martyrs were too little known in Ireland to justify the usual term of martyrology), this circle of biographies was the spiritual reading of the monks, and the familiar instruction of the surrounding people. Several of these *festilogies* are in verse, one of which, the most famous of all, is attributed to Angus, called the *Culdee*, a simple brother, miller of the Monastery of Tallach. In this the principal saints of other countries find a place along with three hundred and sixty-five Irish saints, one for each day of the year, who are all celebrated with that pious and patriotic enthusiasm, at once poetical and moral, which burns so naturally in every Irish heart.

The name of Culdee leads us to point out in

passing the absurd and widespread error which has made the Culdees be looked upon as a kind of monkish order, married and indigenous to the soil, which existed before the introduction of Christianity into Ireland and Scotland by the Roman missionaries, and of whom the great abbot of Iona was the founder or chief. This opinion, propagated by learned Anglicans, and blindly copied by various French writers, is now universally acknowledged as false by sincere and competent judges. The Culdees, a sort of third order, attached to the regular monasteries, appeared in Ireland, as elsewhere, only in the ninth century, and had never anything more than a trifling connection with the Columban communities.

Still more striking than the intellectual development of which the Irish monasteries were at this period the centre, is the prodigious activity displayed by the Irish monks in extending and multiplying themselves over all the countries of Europe —here to create new schools and sanctuaries among nations already evangelised—there to carry the light of the Gospel, at peril of their lives, to the countries that were still pagan. We should run the risk of forestalling our future task if we did not resist the temptations of the subject, which would lead us to go faster than time, and to follow those armies of brave and untiring Celts, always adventurous and often heroic, into the regions where we shall perhaps one day find them again. Let us content ourselves with a simple list, which has a certain eloquence even in the dryness of its figures. Here is the number, probably very incomplete, given by an ancient writer, of the monasteries founded out of Ireland by Irish monks, led far from their country by the love of souls, and, no doubt, a little also by that love of travel which has always been one of their special distinctions:—

>Thirteen in Scotland,
>Twelve in England,
>Seven in France,
>Twelve in Armorica,
>Seven in Lorraine,
>Ten in Alsatia,
>Sixteen in Bavaria,
>Fifteen in Rhætia, Helvetia, and Allemania;

without counting many in Thuringia and upon the left bank of the Lower Rhine; and, finally, six in Italy.

And that it may be fully apparent how great was the zeal and virtue of which those monastic colonies were at once the product and the centre, let us place by its side an analogous list of saints of Irish origin, whom the gratitude of nations converted, edified, and civilised by them, have placed upon their altars as patrons and founders of those churches whose foundations they watered with their blood:—

>A hundred and fifty (of whom thirty-six were martyrs) in Germany,
>Forty-five (of whom six were martyrs) in Gaul,

Thirty in Belgium,
Thirteen in Italy,
Eight, all martyrs, in Norway and Iceland.

In the after part of this narrative we shall meet many of the most illustrious, especially in Germany. Let us confine ourselves here to pointing out, among the thirteen Irish saints honoured with public veneration in Italy, him who is still invoked at the extremity of the peninsula as the patron of Tarento under the name of San Cataldo.

His name in Ireland was Cathal, and before he left his country to go on a pilgrimage to Jerusalem, and to become a bishop at Tarento, he had presided over the great monastic school of Lismore, in the south of Ireland. Thanks to his zeal and knowledge, this school had become a sort of university, to which he attracted an immense crowd of students, not only Irish, but foreigners, from Wales, England, France, and even from Germany. When their education was concluded, a portion of them remained to increase the already numerous communities in the holy and lettered city of Lismore; the others carried back with them to their different countries a recollection of the advantages which they owed to Ireland and her monks. For it is important to prove that, while Ireland sent forth her sons into all the regions of the then known world, numberless strangers hastened there to seat themselves at the feet of her doctors, and to find in that vast centre of faith and knowledge all the remnants of ancient civilisation which her insular position had permitted her to save from the flood of barbarous invasions.

The monasteries which gradually covered the soil of Ireland were thus the hostelries of a foreign emigration. Unlike the ancient Druidical colleges, they were open to all. The poor and the rich, the slave as well as the freeman, the child and the old man, had free access and paid nothing. It was not, then, only to the natives of Ireland that the Irish monasteries, occupied and ruled by the sons of Columba, confined the benefits of knowledge and of literary and religious education. They opened their door with admirable generosity to strangers from every country and of every condition; above all, to those who came from the neighbouring island, England, some to end their lives in an Irish cloister, some to search from house to house for books, and masters capable of explaining those books. The Irish monks received with kindness guests so greedy of instruction, and gave them both books and masters, the food of the body and the food of the soul, without demanding any recompense. The Anglo-Saxons, who were afterwards to repay this teaching with ingratitude so cruel, were of all nations the one which derived most profit from it. From the seventh to the eleventh century English students flocked into Ireland, and for four hundred years the monastic schools of the island maintained the great reputation which brought so many successive generations to dip deeply there into the living waters of knowledge and of faith.

This devotion to knowledge and generous munificence towards strangers, this studious and intellectual life, nourished into being by the sheltering warmth of faith, shone with all the more brightness amid the horrible confusion and bloody disasters which signalise, in so far as concerned temporal affairs, the *Golden Age* of ecclesiastical history in Ireland, even before the sanguinary invasions of the Danes at the end of the eighth century. It has been said with justice that war and religion have been in all ages the two great passions of Ireland. But it must be allowed that war seems almost always to have carried the day over religion, and that religion did not prevent war from degenerating too often into massacres and assassinations. It is true that after the eighth century there are fewer kings murdered by their successors than in the period between St Patrick and St Columba; it is true that three or four of these kings lived long enough to have the time to go and expiate their sins as monks at Armagh or Iona. But it is not less true that the annals of the monastic family of Columba present to us at each line with mournful laconism a spectacle which absolutely contradicts the flattering pictures which have been drawn of the peace which Ireland should have enjoyed. Almost every year, such words as the following are repeated with cruel brevity:—

> *Bellum.*
> *Bellum lacrymabile.*
> *Bellum magnum.*
> *Vastatio.*
> *Spoliatio.*
> *Violatio.*
> *Obsessio.*
> *Strages magna.*
> *Jugulatio.*

And above all, *Jugulatio.* It is the word which returns oftenest, and in which seems to be summed up the destiny of those unhappy princes and people.

Such an enumeration should give rise to the reflection, what this wild tree of Celtic nature would have been without the monastic graft. We can thus perceive with what ferocious natures Columba and his disciples had to do. If, notwithstanding the preaching of the monks, a state of affairs so barbarous continued to exist, what might it have been had the Gospel never been preached to those savages, and if the monks had not been in the midst of them like a permanent incarnation of the Spirit of God?

The monks were at the same time neither less inactive nor more spared than the women, who fought and perished in the wars precisely like the men, up to the time when the most illustrious of Columba's successors delivered them from that terrible bondage. A single incident drawn from the sanguinary chaos of the period will suffice at once to paint the always atrocious habits of those Celtic Christians, and the always beneficent influence of monastic authority. A hundred years after the death of Columba, his biographer and ninth successor, Adamnan, was crossing a plain, carrying his old mother on his back, when they saw two bands fighting, and in the midst of the battle a woman dragging another woman after her, whose breast she had pierced with an iron hook. At this horrible spectacle the abbot's mother seated herself on the ground, and said to him, " I will not leave this spot till thou hast promised me to have women exempted for ever from this horror, and from every battle and expedition." He gave her his word, and he kept it. At the next national assembly of Tara, he proposed and carried a law which is inscribed in the annals of Ireland as the *Law of Adamnan*, or *Law of the Innocents*, and which for ever freed the Irish women from the obligation of military service and all its homicidal consequences.

At the same time, nothing was more common in Ireland than the armed intervention of the monks in civil wars, or in the struggles between different communities. We may be permitted to believe that the spiritual descendants of Columba reckoned among them more than one monk of character as warlike as their great ancestor, and that there were as many monastic actors as victims in these desperate conflicts. Two centuries after Columba, two hundred monks of his abbey at Durrow perished in a battle with the neighbouring monks of Clonmacnoise; and the old annalists of Ireland speak of a battle which took place in 816, at which eight hundred monks of Ferns were killed. The Irish religious had not given up either the warlike humour or the dauntless courage of their race.

Nor is it less certain that the studious fervour and persevering patriotism which were such marked features in the character of Columba remained the inalienable inheritance of his monastic posterity—an inheritance which continued up to the middle ages, to the time of that famous statute of Kilkenny, which is an ineffaceable monument of the ferocious arrogance of the English conquerors, even before the Reformation. This statute, after having denounced every marriage between the two races as an act of high treason, went so far as to exclude all native Irish from the monasteries—from those same monasteries which Irishmen alone had founded and occupied for eight centuries, and where, before and after Columba, they had afforded a generous hospitality to the British fugitives and to the victorious Saxons.

But we must not permit ourselves to linger on the Irish coasts. We shall soon again meet her generous and intrepid sons, always the first in the field, and the most ready to expose themselves to danger, among the apostles and propagators of monastic institutions, upon the banks of the Scheldt, the Rhine, and the Danube, where also they were eclipsed and surpassed by the Anglo-Saxons, but where their names, forgotten in Ireland, still shine with a pure and beneficent light.

The influence of Columba, so universal, undeniable, and enduring in his native island, should not have been less so in his adopted country—in that Caledonia which became more and more an Irish or Scotic colony, and thus merited the name of Scotland, which it retained. Notwithstanding, his work has perhaps left fewer authentic traces there. All unite in attributing to him the conversion of the Northern Picts, and the introduction or re-establishment of the faith among the Picts of the South and the Scots of the West. It is also pretty generally agreed to date from his times—even though there is no evidence of their direct subordination to Iona—the great monasteries of Old Melrose, of Abercorn, Tynninghame, and Coldingham, situated between the Forth and the Tweed, and which afterwards became the centres of Christian extension among the Saxons of Northumbria. Further north, but still upon the east coast, the round towers which are still to be seen at Brechin and Abernethy bear witness to their Irish origin, and consequently to the influence of Columba, who was the first and principal Irish missionary in these districts. The same may be said of those primitive and lowly constructions built with long and large stones laid upon each other, without cement, which are to be found in St Kilda and other Hebridean isles, and also upon certain points of the neighbouring shore, resembling exactly in form the deserted monasteries which are so numerous in the isles of western Ireland. Another relic of the primitive Church is found in the caves, hollowed out or enlarged by the hand of man, in the cliffs or mountains of the interior, inhabited of old, as were the grots of Subiaco and Marmoutier, and as the caves of Meteores in Albania are still, by hermits, or sometimes even by bishops (as St Woloc, St Regulus). Kentigern, the apostle of Strathclyde, appears to us in the legend at the mouth of his episcopal cave, which was hollowed out in the side of a cliff, and where the people looked at him from afar with respectful curiosity, while he studied the direction of the storms at sea, and breathed in with pleasure the first breezes of the spring.

This bishop, Welsh by birth, has already been mentioned in connection with the principality of Wales, where, as we have already seen, he founded an immense monastery during an exile, the cause of which it is impossible to ascertain, but which was the occasion of a relapse into idolatry among his diocesans. The district of Strathclyde or Cumbria, on the west coasts of Britain, from the mouth of the Clyde to that of the Mersey—that is to say, from Glasgow to Liverpool—was occupied by a mingled race of Britons and Scots, whose capital was Al-Cluid, now Dumbarton. A prince called Roderick (Rydderch Haël), whose mother was Irish, and who had been baptised by an Irish monk, hastened, when the authority fell into his hands, to recall Kentigern, who returned bringing with him a hive of Welsh monks, and established definitively the seat of his apostleship at Glasgow, where Ninian had preceded him nearly a century before without leaving any lasting traces of his passage. Kentigern, more fortunate, established upon the site of a burying-ground consecrated by Ninian the first foundation of the magnificent cathedral which still bears his name.

It was consecrated by an Irish bishop, brought from Ireland for the purpose, and who celebrated that ceremony without the assistance of other bishops, according to Celtic customs. Kentigern collected round him numerous disciples, all learned in holy literature, all working with their hands, and possessing nothing as individuals—a true monastic community. He distinguished himself during all his episcopate by his efforts to bring back to the faith the Picts of Galloway, which formed part of the kingdom of Strathclyde; and afterwards by numerous missions and monastic foundations throughout all Albyn—a name which was then given to midland Scotland. His disciples penetrated even to the Orkney Isles, where they must have met with the missionaries of Iona.

The salutary and laborious activity of Kentigern

must often have encroached upon the regions which were specially within the sphere of Columba. But the generous heart of Columba was inaccessible to jealousy. He was besides the personal friend of Kentigern and of King Roderick. The fame of the Bishop of Strathclyde's apostolic labours drew him from his isle to do homage to his rival. He arrived from Iona with a great train of monks, whom he arranged in three companies at the moment of their entrance into Glasgow. Kentigern distributed in the same way the numerous monks who surrounded him in his episcopal monastery, and whom he led out to meet the abbot of Iona. He divided them, according to their age, into three bands, the youngest of whom marched first; then those who had reached the age of manhood; and, last of all, the old and grey-haired, among whom he himself took his place. They all chanted the anthem, *In viis Domini magna est gloria Domini, et via justorum facta est: et iter sanctorum præparatum est.* The monks of Iona, on their side, chanted in choir the versicle, *Ibunt sancti de virtute in virtutem: videbitur Deus eorum in Sion.* From each side echoed the Alleluia; and it was to the sound of those words of Holy Scripture, chanted in Latin by the Celtic monks of Wales and Ireland, that the two apostles of the Picts and Scots met at what had been the extreme boundary of the Roman Empire and limit of the power of the Cæsars, and upon a soil henceforth for ever freed from paganism and idolatry.

They embraced each other tenderly, and passed several days in intimate and friendly intercourse.

The historian who has preserved for us the account of this interview does not conceal a less edifying incident. He confesses that some robbers had joined themselves to the following of the abbot of Iona, and that they took advantage of the general enthusiasm to steal a ram from the bishop's flock. They were soon taken; but Kentigern pardoned them. Columba and his fellow-apostle exchanged their pastoral crosses before they parted in token of mutual affection. Another annalist describes them as living together for six months in the monastery which Columba had just founded at Dunkeld, and together preaching the faith to the inhabitants of Athol and the mountainous regions inhabited by the Picts.

I know not how far we may put faith in another narrative of the same author, which seems rather borrowed from the Gallo-Breton epic of Tristan and Iseult than from monastic legend, but which has nevertheless remained Kentigern's most popular title to fame. The wife of King Roderick, led astray by a guilty passion for a knight of her husband's court, had the weakness to bestow upon him a ring which had been given to her by the king. When Roderick was out hunting with this knight, the two took refuge on the banks of the Clyde during the heat of the day, and the knight, falling asleep, unwittingly stretched out his hand, upon which the king saw the ring which he had given to the queen as a token of his love. It was with difficulty that he restrained himself from killing the knight on the spot; but he subdued his rage, and contented himself by taking the ring from his finger and throwing it into the river, without awakening the guilty sleeper. When he had returned to the town he demanded his ring from the queen, and, as she could not produce it, threw her into prison, and gave orders for her execution. She obtained, however, a delay of three days; and having in vain sought the ring from the knight to whom she had given it, she had recourse to the protection of St Kentigern. The good pastor knew or divined all —the ring, found in a salmon which he had caught in the Clyde, was already in his hands. He sent it to the queen, who showed it to her husband, and thus escaped the punishment which awaited her. Roderick even asked her pardon on his knees, and offered to punish her accusers. From this, however, she dissuaded him, and, hastening to Kentigern, confessed her fault to him, and was commanded to pass the rest of her life in penitence. It is for this reason that the ancient effigies of the apostle of Strathclyde represent him as holding always the episcopal cross in one hand, and in the other a salmon with a ring in its mouth.

But neither Kentigern, whose labours can scarcely be said to have survived him, nor Columba, whose influence upon the Picts and Scots was so powerful and lasting, exercised any direct or efficacious action upon the Anglo-Saxons, who became stronger and more formidable from day to day, and whose ferocious incursions threatened the Caledonian tribes no less than the Britons. It is apparent, however, that the great abbot of Iona did not share the repugnance, which had hardened into a system of repulsion, of the Welsh clergy for the Saxon race: express mention, on the contrary, is made in the most authentic documents connected with his history, of Saxon monks who had been admitted into the community of Iona. One of them, for instance, had the office of baker there, and was reckoned among Columba's intimates. But nothing indicates that these Saxons, who were enrolled under the authority of Columba, exercised any influence from thence upon their countrymen. On the contrary, while the Scotic-Briton missionaries spread over all the corners of Caledonia, and while Columba and his disciples carried the light of the Gospel into the northern districts where it had never penetrated, the Christian faith and the Catholic Church languished and gave up the ghost in the southern part of the island under the ruins heaped up everywhere by the Saxon conquest.

Paganism and barbarism, vanquished by the Gospel in the Highlands of the north, again arose and triumphed in the south—in the most populous, accessible, and flourishing districts—throughout all that country, which was destined hereafter to play so great a part in the world, and which already began to call itself England. From 569 to 586—ten years before the death of Columba, and at the period when his authority was best established and most powerful in the north—the last champions of Christian Britain were finally cast out beyond the Severn, while at the same time new bands of Anglo-Saxons in the north, driving back the Picts to the other side of the Tweed, and crossing the Humber to the south, founded the future kingdoms of Mercia and Northumbria. It is true that at a later period the sons of Columba carried the Gospel to those Northumbrians and Mercians. But at the end of the sixth century, after a hundred and fifty years of triumphant invasions and struggles, the Saxons had not yet encountered in any of the then Christian, or at least converted nations (Britons, Scots, and Picts), which they had assailed, fought, and vanquished, either missionaries disposed to announce the good news to them, nor priests capable of maintaining the precious nucleus of faith among the conquered races. In 586 the two last bishops of conquered Britain, those of London and York, abandoned their churches and took refuge in the mountains of Wales, carrying with them the sacred vessels and holy relics which they had been able to save from the rapacity of the idolaters. Other husbandmen were then necessary. From whence were they to come? From the same inextinguishable centre, whence light had been brought to the Irish by Patrick, and to the Britons and Scots by Palladius, Ninian, and Germain.

And already they are here! At the moment when Columba approached the term of his long career in his northern isle, a year before his death, the envoys of Gregory the Great left Rome, and landed, where Cæsar had landed, upon the English shore.

THE END.

www.ingramcontent.com/pod-product-compliance
Lightning Source LLC
Chambersburg PA
CBHW020248170426
43202CB00008B/280